SHELTON STATE
COLLEGE
JUNIOR COLLEGE DIVISION
LIBRARY

W9-DFQ-821

DS
36.7
.A7

The Arab world

DISCARDED

DATE DUE			
MAY 3 1993			
NOV 18 1996			
DEC 0 9 1999			

DS
36.7
.A7

THE
ARAB DISCARDED
WORLD

edited by IRWIN ISENBERG

THE REFERENCE SHELF
Volume 48 Number 2

THE H. W. WILSON COMPANY

New York 1976

THE REFERENCE SHELF

The books in this series contain reprints of articles, excerpts from books, and addresses on current issues and social trends in the United States and other countries. There are six separately bound numbers in each volume, all of which are generally published in the same calendar year. One number is a collection of recent speeches; each of the others is devoted to a single subject and gives background information and discussion from various points of view, concluding with a comprehensive bibliography. Books in the series may be purchased individually or on subscription.

Copyright © 1976
By The H. W. Wilson Company
PRINTED IN THE UNITED STATES OF AMERICA

Library of Congress Cataloging in Publication Data
Main entry under title:

The Arab world.

(The Reference shelf ; v. 48, no. 2)
Bibliography: p.
1. Arab countries. I. Isenberg, Irwin.
II. Series.
DS36.7.A7   909'.09'74927   76–8872
ISBN 0–8242–0596–0

PREFACE

The Arab peoples have a long and proud history. In past centuries they created great empires, built centers of civilization and learning, and made brilliant contributions in the arts and sciences. In recent times, however, the Arab world has been in political disarray and has suffered through prolonged periods of violence.

The Arab world today includes such diverse countries as Egypt, Jordan, Syria, Lebanon, Iraq, Saudi Arabia, Sudan, Algeria, Morocco, and Tunisia, as well as a number of smaller nations. Within this vast territory are cosmopolitan cities such as Cairo in Egypt and Beirut in Lebanon, but much of the area is desert and a majority of the people live in villages. Though the Arab countries have ambitious development plans and some spectacular projects such as Egypt's giant Aswan Dam have been completed, economic progress in the region as a whole has been slow. While there are great concentrations of wealth, based chiefly on oil production, most people live in poverty and have inadequate educational, sanitary, medical, and other services.

For much of the past thirty years the Arab world has been in turmoil. Some Arab countries, such as Algeria, have been torn by revolution; other countries, such as Egypt and Libya, have overthrown corrupt or inept governments and have tried to establish new economic and social orders. Sudan was ripped for years by a devastating civil war. Syria and Iraq have been plagued by unstable governments. Political figures in the Arab world have been targets of assassins. As recently as 1975, King Faisal of Saudi Arabia was gunned down in his own court. Jordan's King Hussein has survived more than twelve attempts on his life. Jordan's prime minister was assassinated in 1970.

The Arab countries have contended with one another on many issues, ranging from conflicting territorial claims to political disagreements to basic differences on world affairs. Dissident groups within countries have been supplied with arms and money by the governments of other countries. Disputes have periodically erupted into pitched battles. For the past year, bloody chaos and a costly civil war have engulfed Lebanon.

Throughout the last three decades, the Arab countries have been in a permanent state of war against Israel. In 1948 (when Israel was created as a homeland for the Jewish people), in 1956, in 1967, and again in 1973, the Arab states and Israel went to war. Though vastly outnumbered, the Israelis gained decisive victories in the first three wars; in 1973, however, the Arab armies made a better showing. A long series of clashes preceded each war and each has been followed by continued deadly skirmishes. The toll in lives has been heavy on both sides.

The Arab-Israeli dispute, which centers on demands for the return of Arab land occupied by Israel and the return of those Arabs—or Palestinians—who left the territory originally designated as Israel, has had worldwide consequences. Arab guerrilla groups have committed acts of terrorism in Israel and in many other countries. Israel has struck back by launching commando raids and bombing attacks against guerrilla camps in neighboring Arab countries.

The United States and the Soviet Union have lined up on opposite sides in this conflict. The United States is an ally of Israel and has supplied it with large quantities of sophisticated weapons. Washington has tried to maintain good relations with the Arab countries, too, and has provided arms to Jordan and Saudi Arabia. It also may give arms to Egypt in the near future. Simultaneously, the United States has been trying to hammer out a peace settlement between the Arab countries and Israel.

The Soviet Union has been friendly to the Arabs and has been the principal supplier of weapons to Egypt, Libya,

Iraq, and Syria. In the last few years, Soviet relations with Egypt have soured, however, while the United States and Egypt have grown more friendly. Throughout this time, the United Nations has been trying to maintain the peace, and UN-sponsored troops have been assigned to buffer zones in several locations to separate the two sides.

Of critical importance to the entire world is the vast amount of oil lying within the Arab countries and beneath their offshore waters. Prior to the 1970s, oil had been a relatively cheap commodity. However, the oil-producing countries had long been asking for more money for their precious natural resource and, in this decade, for the first time they forged a unified position that enabled them to raise prices. In 1973 alone, after the Arab-Israeli war, the price quadrupled. The Arab countries also slashed their oil production by 30 percent to show their displeasure at the pro-Israeli policies of Western countries and even cut off oil supplies completely to the Netherlands for a time. The price rises and the production cutback were stunning blows to oil-importing countries in all parts of the world. In the United States, every household has been hit with sharply higher costs for heating oil, gas, and other petroleum-based products.

At the same time, the hugely increased revenues flowing into the oil-producing countries altered the world's financial balance. With tens of billions of added dollars pouring into their treasuries annually, the Arab governments are investing in Western industry and real estate, lending hundreds of millions of dollars to Moslem countries around the world, and spending heavily on development projects in their own countries.

This volume offers a view of the major interconnected trends and issues in the Arab world today. The first section offers a discussion of the history and geography of the region, a diversified area despite the ethnic, religious, and linguistic bonds of the inhabitants. The second section presents articles highlighting factors that divide the Arab world. Although the prevailing Islamic religion and the possession of oil are powerful cohesive forces, political differences continue to split the countries of the Middle East. One of the most bitter divisions is caused by the differing attitudes toward Israel, with some countries favoring a more conciliatory policy and some a more militant one.

The third section looks at the Middle East as a whole, and at a number of countries in particular, in terms of what is happening economically and politically. Included in this section is an article on the region's dominant military power—Iran—a Moslem, though non-Arab, nation and one associated with the Arabs as an oil-producing state.

The fourth section examines the Arab-Israeli conflict and notes some of the recent events that have occurred in the search for a settlement. The articles in this section convey a sense of the great difficulty that exists in reaching any lasting solution acceptable to both sides. The last section of this volume looks at the Arab countries and their relations with the two world superpowers, the United States and the Soviet Union.

The editor wishes to thank the publishers who have granted permission to reprint the articles in this book.

Irwin Isenberg

March 1976

CONTENTS

I. THE ARAB LANDS, THE ARAB PEOPLE: AN OVERVIEW

EDITOR'S INTRODUCTION

The Middle East is generally thought to be a predominantly Arabic region. This concept requires qualification, however, for the term *Arab* itself is not strictly definable. In a purely semantic sense, no people can be classified as *Arab*, for the word connotes a mixed population with widely varying physical characteristics and racial origins. The word is best used in a cultural context: Arab countries are those in which the primary language is Arabic and the religion Islam. In this sense, the Middle East is primarily an Arab world, a world that reflects one of the most amazing achievements in history—the development and growth of Islam from a local religious phenomenon into a vast sphere of influence and a civilization itself.

The first article in this section provides a historical overview of the Arab region, from pre-Islamic times to the modern era. The second selection discusses the region in terms of its diversities: the lands, peoples, and religions of the Middle East. It is a predominantly desert world inhabited chiefly by Moslem Arabs, but there exist numerous differences that contribute to the dynamics of the area.

The final article offers a personalized account of Islam and what it means to its adherents. Islam, as the article indicates, is more than a formal religion to be routinely observed. It is, as has often been said, a way of life.

ARAB HISTORY [1]

Pre-Islamic Arabia was largely a tribal, grazing society of . . . [people] worshipping gods seen and unseen, in the

[1] From *A Note on the Arab World*, report by Charles F. Gallagher, staff member. '61. American Universities Field Staff. (Southwest Asia Series, v 10, no 8) p. 14-19. Copyright © 1961 by American Universities Field Staff, Inc. 535 Fifth Ave. New York 10017. Reprinted by permission of the publisher.

sky, in objects, and in nature. Its economy was based on its flocks, the horse, and the camel; trade was fostered by the introduction of the last. Where water was permanent and abundant cities came into being; such were Mecca and Medina . . . , which served as meeting places for the caravans and a base for the merchants who conducted the trade. An intimate relationship between the country and the city existed, from each of which the Arabs have drawn much. . . .

In the so-called Dark Age just before Mohammed (roughly 300-600 A.D.) trade withered and the oasis towns declined, partly because of shifts in trade patterns between Rome, Byzantium, and the East. Mecca was saved by having a permanent spring, the *ka'bah*, as a holy site for pilgrims, and its central location. Mohammed was born there around 570 A.D. and, as has been said, succeeded as much because he was a Meccan as anything else. He was first a merchant and then a prophet, but the results of his activities in the latter domain far exceeded any local or regional bounds.

Mohammed received the Word of God, as incorporated in the *Koran*, the holy book of Islam, in his fortieth year, in 610. For the following decade he endeavored to spread this truth to his neighbors with little success. In 622 he and a few hundred followers, persecuted in their home town, journeyed secretly to nearby Yathrib, thenceforth called Medina (Al Madīnah, "The City") where he began to organize the first community of believers . . .

Rise of Islam

By the time of Mohammed's death in 632 his followers were masters of much of the peninsula, and exactly a century later Arab-Moslem armies were fighting the Franks in the heart of France at Poitiers, and had marched to the Indus River in the East. . . . The new caliphate was the most extensive state since Rome, but unlike any previous empire it was a religious state which had come into being under the banner of a reformist faith which proclaimed itself the "seal" and the perfection of previous Jewish and Christian misformations of the truth. *Islām dawlah wa din* (Islam is a state and a

religion) was its foremost tenet, and its ruler was the over-
seer of God on earth. Although practice has varied considerably at times, Islam has never lost its reform character; indeed, it keeps renewing itself periodically by new waves of
purification, and the problem of the definition of state and
religion in modern terms continues, despite the apologetics
of many modern Arab writers, to beset most Arab states.

With the establishment of the caliphate, Islam became
the central fact of Arab life; it has been well put that since
then it is as impossible to think of the Arabs without Islam
as it is to imagine Islam without the Arabs. For the Arabs
themselves, the first years after the conquest brought an
accretion of Greek and Persian thought, contacts with the
Western world through war, trade, and later the Crusades,
and an exchange of values in which the Jewish minority,
especially in Moslem Spain, played a large role.

As the universal Arab state became more cosmopolitan, it
became physically less Arab (but not less Moslem). The
Arabs were a minority in the new world they had made, but
they passed on to the new Moslems in their empire, if not
their Arab blood, the quality of their Arabness. In this
formative period the great cities of the modern Arab world
[Cairo and Baghdad] were born . . . or refurbished with a
new brilliance (Damascus and Tunis, the heir of Carthage).
It is worth noting that the spread of Islam exceeded the
spread of Arabic as a language—the latter prospered in general only where a Semitic or Hamitic tongue had formerly
existed—and that the extension of Arabic was far greater
than colonization by the Arabs themselves. North Africa was
conquered by a handful, and only sparsely settled in the
cities, until the tribal migrations of the eleventh and twelfth
centuries brought a number of rural Arabs into the area.
The fact that Spain received only a sprinkling of Arab
blood (most of the Spanish Moslems were of original penin-
sular stock, plus some Berbers) may in the end have been
the decisive straw that made the Christian reconquest possible.

The six centuries . . . ending in 1258 were, despite an

intellectual apogee in the tenth century, a period of fairly steady political breakdown in which fragmentation gradually overcame unity. Spain was the first to go . . . , next Morocco, then all of North Africa, and finally Egypt. The split-up into petty principalities and the wars and intrigues should not, however, obscure the continuing development of a unified Arab urban civilization which made it possible then and later for scholars and travelers . . . to be equally at home in Fez, Tunis, Cairo, Damascus, or Mecca. That this is still true . . . is one of the pillars of the Arab nationalist renaissance.

Before 1258 the Baghdad caliphate was nominally Arab; after the Mongol invasions destroyed the city it ceased even to be that. The period from the mid-thirteenth to the end of the eighteenth centuries is often referred to by historians as the Arab Decline. In many ways this is true—an inferior quality is noticeable in the bulk of the literature, the arts, and sciences. But it was also the time of the rise of non-Arab Moslems to domination. The Seljuk Turks had already come, and the Ottomans followed them; by the second half of the sixteenth century they controlled all the present Arab area except for Morocco and parts of the southern fringe of [Saudi] Arabia. The rude Turkish character was somewhat planed down by contact with the more civilized Arabs, but the Turks themselves left a deep mark . . .

Probably the most important historical effect of Turkish hegemony was the isolation imposed on the Arabs while the Ottoman Empire faced the European powers at Vienna, in the Balkans, and in southern Russia. The Arabs were placed behind a kind of protective curtain, and from the remoteness of the Arabian heartland at this time sprang the Wahhabi revival movement, . . . represented in the ruling families of Saudi Arabia and Libya. Also from this period dates the spread of the popular brotherhoods, organizations which in some Arab areas have taken on . . . important political colorations. In sum, during these centuries the Arabs lived a cocoonlike existence, returning once again to

the sources for a purer, fresher, popularized, and revitalized
faith, keeping their common language, their customs, and
their unspoken sense of identity. It remained for the dy-
namic Western world to come to their door with the awakening knock. . . .

West Meets East

The use of the cutoff date of 1798 to mark the beginning
of modern Arab history and life is convenient and probably
more valid than most similar dates. The coming of Europe
to the Middle East at the beginning of the 1800s started
changes in Arab existence of a kind that, although still un-
finished, certainly seem permanent. The European influence of our times is comparable to the Hellenistic impression made on earlier Arabs, with the difference that Western
thought and technique continue to progress and develop as
they are being absorbed, while with Greek ideas and science
the Arabs had been able to digest without undue haste a
unitary civilization already complete.

The impact of the West on the Arabs . . . has been intellectual, political, and socioeconomic—roughly in that chron-
ological sequence (but not in ultimate importance). The first
stirrings of the Arab revival were significantly literary: to
reform the ossified classical language so as to prepare it for
the dual task of understanding the Arab past and transmit-
ting the new values of Western thought. Gradually the first
travelers' accounts and the catalogs of Western marvels gave
way to essays on what made the Occident prosperous and
powerful. With these inquiries entered the ideas of nationality, patriotism, and citizenship—terms at first almost un-
translatable—and they became common currency later in the
century, in the 1880s. The idea of being an "Arab" instead
of a resident of Damascus, a Druze, a Sunni Moslem, or an
Orthodox Christian, a tanner or a carpenter, began to make
headway. . . .

But the West was not satisfied to export only its liberal,
nationalist philosophy. With it went the concept of the

white man's burden and the secular civilizing crusade, the
missionary spirit, plus the demands of the burgeoning industrial revolution for raw materials, markets, and labor, and
the power rivalry for strategic places. Penetration of the
Arab world began as early as 1830 in Algeria—the first to be
taken is the last to be released—and with the occupation of
the coaling station of Aden in 1839. The critical point in
Arab-Western relations turned on the occupation of Egypt
in 1881, after the building of the Suez Canal had made that
country a more important pivot than ever in the eastern
trade. British forces were in Egypt for seventy-three years,
and the canal zone was evacuated only in 1954 . . .

By the beginning of World War I, European powers
held the whole North African coast: France in Morocco,
Algeria, and Tunisia; Italy in Libya; Britain in Egypt.
Paradoxically the British occupation of Egypt allowed Arab
nationalists to flourish there outside the jurisdiction of the
Ottoman government, and at the beginning of this century
Cairo had replaced Beirut as the intellectual center of the
Arab renaissance. The Arabs in Asia chafed under the
Turkish yoke and, prodded and promised by British diplomacy during the First World War, rose in a successful
rebellion on the Allied side (1916-1918), only to have the
expected fruits of victory denied them in the peace settlements of 1920. In this Year of Disaster as it is known, the
former provinces of the Turkish Empire in Asia were
handed out as mandates to England and France. Britain
took Palestine and Iraq, and set up an artificial desert emir-
ate in Transjordan to accommodate another of its favor-
ites; France took control in Syria and an enlarged Lebanon.
Except for the interior of the Arabian peninsula, the Arab
world was . . . wholly subject to the rule of foreigners and
infidels.

The consequences of these decisions were and still are
dramatic. The map of the Arab world was set in a mold
which is difficult to change and the Arab personality was
deeply scarred. The [British] Balfour Declaration of 1917

. . . [which favored the establishment of] a national home for Jews in Palestine had aroused the Arabs, and interwar Zionist immigration into . . . [Palestine] rubbed salt into the wounds. The Arabs were psychologically gravely wounded by being told they were not fit to govern themselves after they had fought for their freedom. They were outraged that part of their homeland was thrown open to settlement by outsiders. They were confused to learn that, now having discovered themselves as Arabs, they must unlearn this and become Iraqis, Jordanians, and Syrians. . . .

[Another] aspect of Western penetration came with the socioeconomic impact; in many ways this has been the most devastating. A useful example is that of Egypt under British rule after 1881. The occupying power rescued the country from bankruptcy, restored the finances to soundness, improved agriculture, regulated the Nile with a series of dams, increased sugar and cotton production, and all in all brought Egypt to a degree of prosperity it had never known before—all this in a generation.

Anti-Western Feelings Emerge

At the end of twenty-five years of British rule, however, a new westernized middle class was arising—teachers, lawyers, civil servants, doctors, and army officers. Cairo became superficially a great European-looking city by 1910. Its modern buildings, Western clothes, European food, broad streets, and railroads were imposing, but they masked the inner revolution that had been going on in education and law. Egypt had already begun to turn out young men who found no positions equal to the learning that had been instilled into them. . . . Meanwhile the Holy Law . . . had begun a gradual retreat before the civil codes of Europe, imported and adapted to the local scene. Parallel to this was a capitulatory system of justice for foreigners which released them from nearly all obligation. Protected by force and the law, the foreigners ruled, dispensed justice among themselves, and in league with the semiforeign pashas and beys and the Turco-Levantine aristocracy which made up court circles and higher society, owned the large businesses, held most of the shares, took most of the profits and sent a goodly share of them abroad. The mass of the fellahin in the countryside and the city workers led their usual drab, hopeless lives, protected, it is true, by a Pax Britannica but surrounded by a society in which they had no real part.

It was the rising minority in the new professional and middle class which saw the system as a whole and decided to remedy it. The goal became to learn to do what the foreigners did, do it as well or better, get rid of them, and prosper nationally in the way they had personally. To the aims of political freedom, and a sense of Arab oneness, these young Egyptian nationalists (and the pattern was later repeated in most Arab countries) had added the demand for social justice. It was men of this type, notably angry young officers with the power of the army behind them—stubborn, single-minded, frustrated, patriotic, ascetic, and deeply rooted in the popular stock—who staged most of the *coups* that shook the Arab world after 1948, culminating in the Egyptian revolution of July 23, 1952.

LANDS, PEOPLES, AND RELIGIONS [2]

Geographical Diversity

The Middle East contains three main geographical regions which cut across national and political divisions. These are the Northern Tier, the Fertile Crescent and the largely desert south.

The Northern Tier, which encompasses Turkey, northern Iraq, and the northern and western sectors of Iran, consists mainly of mountains and semiarid plateaus. Like parts of our own West, much of the Northern Tier depends both on

[2] From *Middle East—National Growing Pains,* pamphlet by John B. Christopher, professor of history, University of Washington. (Headline Series no 148) Foreign Policy Association. '61. p 5-15. Reprinted by permission. Copyright, 1961 by Foreign Policy Association, Inc. 345 E. 46th St. New York 10017.

irrigation and on the relatively light rainfall to support agriculture. The chief exceptions to the prevailing dryness are
the narrow band of Iranian territory along the Caspian Sea
and the coastal perimeter of Turkey, especially along the
Black Sea.

The Fertile Crescent forms the southern border of the
Northern Tier. It stretches northward through Israel and
Lebanon, then arcs across northern Syria to the valleys of
the Euphrates and Tigris rivers in Iraq. The Fertile Crescent
has a marked resemblance to southern California, with
bare, brown mountains, productive plains, and the climatic
rhythm of winter rains and summer drought. The Fertile
Crescent has supported a relatively large population since
the remotest days of antiquity. But the area itself is small;
for example, a two-hour drive takes one from the orange
groves of coastal Israel to the desolation of the Dead Sea.

Deserts—and Oases

The largest geographical region comprises the deserts
and oases lying east and south of the Fertile Crescent. The
deserts that cover most of the region vary in character from
the undulating sands of western Egypt and southeastern
[Saudi] Arabia to the rocky wilderness of eastern Egypt, the
ghastly salt flats in the heart of Iran and the relatively hos-
pitable steppe desert of Syria. Except in the well-watered
highlands of Yemen, rainfall is quite inadequate for agriculture. During the long summer, the heat is intense; in the
cities of Iraq and the Persian Gulf temperatures of 110° to
120° [Fahrenheit] are commonplace.

According to a Western stereotype, this is the land of the
Bedouin, the nomads forever seeking pasture for their flocks.
It is true that the nomads, while few in number, have left a
strong tradition. But the stereotype can be misleading, for
most Arabs are farmers and townspeople, settled wherever
there is enough water to support life. The core of this
Middle Eastern south lies in its teeming oases, the greatest
of which are the valleys of the Tigris and Euphrates and,

above all, the Nile. For more than five thousand years Egyptians have lived and died, not on the nearly 400,000 square miles recorded as theirs in statistical tables, but on the few thousand square miles stretching like a green ribbon along the Nile.

Limited Natural Resources

The total of Middle Eastern natural resources is not impressive. The majority of Middle Easterners are farmers, yet the bulk of the land is unfit for agricultural use. With the irrigation facilities . . . available, only . . . [20] percent of the whole area can grow crops, although some additional marginal lands are used for pasture. These basic facts explain why the Middle East must be reckoned among the impoverished and underdeveloped sections of the world.

But surely oil is revolutionizing the Middle Eastern economy? . . . [The area] contains over two thirds of all known reserves of petroleum. Costs of production are very low, because the oil flows from a few large wells rather than many small ones, and the presence of natural gas makes expensive pumping installations unnecessary. Yet . . . this oil wealth has benefited only a fraction of the population.

A Human Melting Pot

The Middle East has been a melting pot of humanity ever since history began. Later invaders and conquerors, as well as countless African Negroes brought in as slaves, have added to an already confused mixture of races. There is, thus, no use in trying to group the inhabitants of the contemporary Middle East according to some racial formula.

It is both possible and useful, however, to group Middle Easterners according to the languages they speak, the religions they profess and the traditions they honor. This pattern shows four major national groups, . . . Turkish, Iranian, Israeli and Arab. The pattern is immensely complicated, however, by the presence of many minorities—minorities by virtue of nationality or religion or language or some combination of the three. The relationship between majority and minority groups is one of the chronic problems of Middle Eastern society.

The Majority Peoples

The Turks are the descendants of the Ottomans who occupied Anatolia (Asia Minor) during the last centuries of the Middle Ages. Their religion is Islam. Their language, although . . . written in the Latin alphabet, is Central Asian in origin; its only relatives in Europe are Finnish and Hungarian. In the Middle East, languages akin to Turkish are spoken by some of the minorities in Iran.

The Iranians, too, are for the most part Moslems. The name "Iran," which was substituted for the traditional "Persia" in the 1930s, means land of the Aryans. While the claim of some Iranians to be of pure Aryan stock is unproved, their language does belong to the great family of Indo-European or Aryan languages, which also includes most of the European tongues. It is called Farsi, and uses the Arabic alphabet.

The Israelis constitute a special case. Religion has been the main element that has kept them intact as a nation over the centuries. . . . Many belong to Orthodox Judaism, others favor separation of church and state and practice secularism. . . . The common denominator of Israeli nationhood, political and emotional in essence, is the determination to maintain a modern Jewish state where the Jews lived in the days of the Old Testament. [Their language, Hebrew, is a Semitic tongue akin to Arabic—Ed.]

The Arabs, the fourth majority group, claim to form a single national group. Most of them profess a common religion, Islam, and all of them speak a common language of which they are immensely proud. Politically, however, the Arabs are divided into a multitude of units ranging from . . . [Egypt] down to the tiny principalities on the Persian Gulf.

National Minorities

The most significant national minorities in the Middle East are the Kurds, the Iranian "tribes" and the Armenians.

The Kurds, who number perhaps . . . [ten] million, are a hardy pastoral people living in the highlands along the upper Tigris River and its tributaries. They are Moslems, and they speak an Indo-European language related to Persian. Kurdistan, as their homeland is termed, is partitioned among four states—Turkey, Iraq, Iran and . . . Syria. . . . These states have long opposed efforts to establish an independent Kurdistan, which would in any event be hard to govern because of the traditional divisions of the Kurds themselves into feuding tribes. . . . The Kurds remain a more or less rebellious minority wherever they are, although some observers believe that they are gradually being assimilated into the dominant majorities. [This is not the case in Iraq, where violent factions of the country's two million Kurds are fighting for an autonomous Kurdish state of their own.—Ed.]

The Iranian "tribes" are a fascinating collection of minorities who make up about . . . [15] percent of the total population of Iran. They include Kurds, Bakhtiaris, Lurs, and still others who are rough mountaineers and differ from the majority of Iranians in their way of life and sometimes in language. They migrate according to a set seasonal pattern and along established routes to pasture their stock. The hardships of migration—among them the need to transport animals by the tens of thousands across raging rivers and snowy mountain passes—have eased very little since they were recorded in *Grass,* a . . . film of the 1920s. The tribesmen have much of the contempt for settled modern ways which we Americans associate with our own Wild West.

The Armenians offer a great contrast to the Iranian "tribes." They are Christian; they speak an Indo-European language with its own distinctive alphabet; and they are primarily urban, working as shopkeepers and craftsmen. A century ago they lived mostly in Turkey, particularly in their historic home near the Russian frontier. Then came Armenian rebellions against Turkish rule and bloody Turkish reprisals, culminating in the Armenian massacres of World War I. After the war the survivors found new homes in the Arab lands to the south. While some of them later joined their kinsmen in the Armenian Soviet Socialist Republic, about 400,000 Armenians remain in the Middle East. . . . Their largest communities are in Beirut [Lebanon] and in the northern Syrian city of Aleppo.

Region of Many Faiths

In the history of the Middle East, religion has probably been the most important issue dividing minorities from majorities. Even . . . "sectarian difficulties," as religious tensions are delicately described, still cause riots and cost lives. This is the reason for the "nervous climate" that observers note among religious minorities.

The majority religion of the Middle East is Islam; the largest minority religion is Christianity. Both have played a role of the first magnitude in shaping the modern Middle East. But there are many other religious minorities—Jews, Druzes, Baha'is, Zoroastrians, "devil worshippers," and still more.

Islam: Religion of Submission

Islam means "submission"—submission to the will of Allah—and its followers call themselves Moslems, "those who have submitted." It was founded by Mohammed, early in the seventh century A.D. Mohammed believed that, whereas God's design had been partially revealed to the prophets of the Old Testament and to Jesus, he himself had received the full revelation. Thus he taught that Jews and Christians should be tolerated, although hardly treated as equals. Here, however, Moslem practice has not always followed Mohammed's teaching.

Many links exist between Islam and its Jewish and Christian forerunners. Islam, too, is monotheistic and preaches the hope of heaven and the fear of hell. Yet Islam also differs markedly from Judaism and Christianity. Contrary to an erroneous Western view, the central difference is not Moslem tolerance of polygamy, for relatively few Moslems can afford to support more than one wife. It is, rather, the relatively greater simplicity of Islam. Islam has no clergy, strictly speaking; Moslems regard Mohammed as a divinely inspired mortal, not as the Son of God, and object, therefore, to being called Mohammedans.

In the early days of Islam, religion and politics were fused together. The caliphs, the successors of Mohammed, were at once secular rulers, religious leaders and supreme judges. The law they enforced was sacred law, based on the revelations of Mohammed compiled in the Koran. Later, this fusion melted away; the caliphate was almost meaningless for centuries before its abolition in the 1920s. The Sacred Law, although still enforced in isolated lands like Saudi Arabia, is yielding ground to man-made law in most of the Middle East.

Islam Not Static

Westerners often find in Islam features which seem hostile to modern concepts of progress and development. The practice of encouraging the young to memorize the Koran by rote is in sharp contrast to Western ideas of education. The submission to God's will as denoted by the word "Islam" seems to foster a fatalistic acceptance of things as they are and to deny the possibility of making things what they should be. Thus some Westerners are apt to assume that Islam is a static faith. Such a conclusion, however, is dangerously misleading. Islam has weathered many crises in the past; and in the future it may well adjust itself to the increasingly rapid changes in Middle Eastern life. Its greatest strength lies in its appeal to the emotions of millions of men and women. Its genuine racial equality is another asset, for Islam is free of the taint of "the white man's burden," which often makes Christianity appear to non-Christians as the instrument of Western racial prejudice and colonialism.

Islamic Sects: Sunni and Shiite

The ability of Islam to accommodate widely differing beliefs and practices is another source of strength. But it is a source of weakness, too, for it has divided Moslems into rival sects. The fundamental cleavage separates Sunni Moslems from . . . [Shiite] Moslems. The Sunnis regard themselves as the upholders of Islamic orthodoxy; in their eyes the . . . [Shiite] Moslems are heretics. The term . . . [Shiite], meaning sect or party, became attached early in Islamic history to the partisans of Ali, the son-in-law of Mohammed and the fourth caliph. As the doctrine of . . . [Shiism] developed, it almost ignored Mohammed and attributed miraculous powers to Ali and his descendants, many of whom were persecuted by the Sunni caliphs.

In most Middle Eastern countries the Sunnis are the predominant Moslem group. In Iran, however, . . . [Shiism] is the state religion and the faith of the majority. In Iraq, where the most sacred . . . [Shiite] shrines are located, its followers comprise almost half the population. Elsewhere, especially in Lebanon and Syria, there are significant . . . [Shiite] communities, frequently at odds with their Sunni neighbors—a good example of the "nervous climate" often affecting minorities.

Christianity: Fragmented Into Sects

Middle Eastern Christendom, too, is divided. There are the Orthodox churches—Greek, Syrian, Armenian, and others. Second, there is the heretical Coptic church, to which the majority of Egyptian Christians belong. Third, there are the Uniat churches, which rejoined Roman Catholicism in return for concessions allowing the marriage of priests and the use of local languages. The Maronite church in Lebanon is the most important Uniat body in the Middle East, though most of the other churches have their Uniat counterparts—Greek Catholic, Armenian Catholic, and so on. Finally, there are a few Protestants, converted by Anglican and American Presbyterian missionaries during the last century and a half.

The total number of Middle Eastern Christians is comparatively small. Even in Lebanon, their stronghold, they make up only slightly more than half the population. [According to recent estimates, the Moslems now constitute about 60 percent of the population.—Ed.] In Syria, the Christians comprise about . . . [10] percent of the population; in Egypt and Jordan, about 7 percent; nowhere else do they exceed 3 percent.

Role of Christians Important

Yet the Christian minorities, because of their long contact with the men and ideas of the West, have played a very significant role as agents of modernization and contributors to awakening nationalism. Christians, more than Moslems, have migrated abroad yet kept in close touch with their relatives back home. Christians, more than Moslems, attended Catholic and Protestant mission schools, and thereby achieved both a higher rate of literacy and a wider knowledge of the world. In turn, when Western businessmen and officials went to the Middle East, they chose Christians rather than Moslems as partners or assistants. . . .

The nationalism that the Christians helped to arouse is often turned against them. Their identification with the West opens them to the charge of guilt by association with imperialism; in the eyes of fervent anticolonialists, they are most imperfect nationalists. The Christians, for their part, claim that their traditional rights are being discriminated against in the filling of government jobs and the awarding of scholarships. These complaints, while often exaggerated to enlist Western sympathy, are well founded. The Christians, like other minorities in the Middle East, live in a "nervous climate."

RELIGION FOR ALL SEASONS [3]

At the Jidda [Saudi Arabia] airport, a dozen Moslem pilgrims descended from the Saudi Arabian Boeing 737 in bright sunshine. All wore the white, seamless garments of *Ihram,* men with a bared shoulder, women looking like nuns in white, fresh from a convent. Identical dress assured that each person would be identical before God on this most holy pilgrimage to Mecca, the *Hajj.*

"*Laa ilaaha illa Allaah,*" called the leader of the group, as his feet touched the tarmac.

"There is no god but Allah," his companion repeated after him.

"*Labayka!*" the leader called out.

Once more his companions repeated after him, "I am at your service, oh Lord."

Umbrellas opened to shield bare heads and shoulders from the strong sun. Together the group trekked toward the immigration counter of the airport.

Once again, the annual *Hajj* was under way. Over a million of the world's 500 million Moslems were traveling to Mecca. Most of them were coming through Jidda, the Red Sea port that is only forty miles from Mecca by a four-lane superhighway.

Arriving ships disgorged passengers at the new harbor set on an island in a bay of the limpid Red Sea. Planes disembarked passengers from as far away as Taiwan, Mauritius, and Morocco. Buses rolled in from Jordan, Iraq, Syria, Lebanon and the sheikdoms of the United Arab Emirates. One rainbowed-colored bus carried a group of Arabs from the Israeli-occupied West Bank of Jordan, a group permitted to depart for the *Hajj* by Israeli authorities.

Few things are more awesome than is the annual *Hajj,*

[3] From *The Kingdom of Oil,* by Ray Vicker, staff reporter of *The Wall Street Journal.* Scribner. '74. p 34-47. Reprinted by permission of Charles Scribner's Sons from *The Kingdom of Oil* by Ray Vicker. Copyright © 1974 by Ray Vicker.

which brings devout Moslems to Mecca and its adjacent sacred places during *Dhu-I-Hijja,* the holy days in the final month of the Moslem year. A frenzy sweeps through the hundreds of thousands of assembling people as the days near. For weeks, people have been arriving, so fearful of travel foul-ups that some come a month ahead of time. Street jams intensify. The highway to Mecca becomes one long line of automobiles, buses, and open trucks with people piled on platforms.

The time is past when camel and donkey trains carried the devout pilgrims those last miles to Mecca. This does not lessen the power of this holy spectacle, which emphasizes the hold Islam has over its adherents. Mohammedanism is an extrovertic religion in its outward manifestations. The devout man thinks nothing of placing a prayer rug, a garment, or a newspaper on the street to pray at the appropriate times while facing Mecca. The speech of the Moslem is interlaced with phrases thanking God for everything, down to the mere fact of being allowed to live. The pilgrimage itself will become a matter of pride for the pilgrim. It will become a part of his official history, like a government decoration or citation for a meritorious task.

Most of the people living in the Middle East are Moslem. Some are strict orthodox. Others are little more than Moslem in name. All regard their religion in a way that sometimes is difficult for the modern Western mind to grasp. Religion in the Middle East is something to be taken seriously, like strong medication to purge the spirit. The Christian may joke about his particular sect, sometimes in a shame-faced manner to hide his true feelings. One seldom hears the Moslem joke about his religion. When Islam comes under attack, all Moslems draw together.

The Koran says: "Fight in the way of Allah against those who fight against you, but begin not hostilities. Lo. Allah loveth not aggressors." In the Yom Kippur War [of 1973], Arabs claimed their first strike was only a return to Arab lands, not an aggression.

Moslemism is more than just a sabbath religion to the devout person. It is part of his life. He lives by the Koran, quoting it extensively in his daily conversation to stress that it is governing his actions:

Never will Allah suffer the reward to be lost of those who do right. [Koran, Yusuf 90]

God is with those who patiently persevere. [Koran, Anfal 46]

Such comments permeate conversations, appear in writings of authors, interlace speeches of politicians and statesmen, and illustrate legal decisions. Saudi Arabia follows principles of Islam in its constitution and in its judicial and governmental system. Libya's fiery leader, Colonel Muammar al Qaddafi, governs Libya according to the precepts of the Koran.

To a lesser extent other Moslem leaders heed the Koran in making decisions and in interpreting situations. It is as if President John F. Kennedy had openly used Catholic doctrine to define his actions in the White House, or as if [former] President Richard M. Nixon were to turn to Quaker precepts to codify his decision making.

Anyone who wants to understand the Middle Easterner, his psychology and his attitudes, should read the Koran and study the religion that has been built about it. Moslems regard the Koran as the word of God, as revealed to the Prophet Mohammed. Note that Mohammed is only a prophet, not the object of worship.

In the Moslem view, if a person incorporates the Koran into his family affairs, his politics, his business, and other aspects of his daily life, he is merely paying attention to the word of God. If someone asks him about that, his response is apt to be, "Shouldn't everybody?"

"Our religion gives us that something more, that something that binds us all together," said Hisham Nazer, Saudi Arabia's minister of state for planning.

Sheik Nazer is articulate, trim, with the air of confidence

of one who has attained power at an early age, and used it well. When I commented that it was unusual to meet a thirty-nine-year-old minister, a smile formed around his moustache and he said, "I was appointed when I was thirty-one."

I had met him in his olive-green-carpeted, mahogany-paneled office in Riyadh, Saudi Arabia's capital, when I was investigating the scope of his country's development program. Sheik Nazar, I had been told, is the man who keeps everything moving in a five-year development program, which is seeing more than $10 billion poured into schools, hospitals, roads, communications networks, and other paraphernalia of a modern civilization.

After he had outlined dozens of major programs aimed at bettering the lot of the ordinary citizen, I had raised the question, "Won't education and material progress encourage citizens to reach for something else, for more political freedom?"

"We already have something else," he said, quietly. "Our religion. We believe that we have the framework for democracy and for the protection of human and political rights in the writings of the Koran. You must never underestimate the power of the religion which holds us together. All the money we are spending for development in this country would mean nothing if we did not have the people with us, a people infused with the spirit of Islam."

This was not exactly the answer one expects to receive from a minister of planning, but it is the sort of answer one finds frequently in a Moslem world. Politics, economic development, and religion are so interwoven that a new mosque may be included along with a hospital and a school in building plans for modernizing a mud-brick village. Saudi Arabia is completing a new industrial zone in the Eastern Province on the edge of Dammam. The minaret of a government-built mosque rises amid the warehouses, the power plant, and other facilities constructed to assist manufacturers who might want to locate there.

During the holy fasting month of Ramadan entire countries sometimes grind to a halt. Offices are deserted or understaffed. Letters are left unanswered, should any be delivered. Shipments of merchandise are delayed. Tasks are postponed. All attention is focused upon complete abstinence from food and drink from sunrise to sunset during this month. This is a difficult task for anyone who might be doing an ordinary day's work. When the crunch comes, the day's work suffers. Sometimes dispositions may suffer too.

Cairo is a teeming, friendly city crowded beside a Nile that still can look romantic, though high-rise monuments of concrete and steel now line the river banks. Normally, Cairene hospitality is as inviting as the tantalizing cooking odors that float from sidewalk restaurants in the Khan el Khalili Bazaar.

But one recent afternoon [in 1974] in the Ramadan a crowd was collecting on Soliman Pasha Street, that thoroughfare which has some of the most exclusive shops in the city. Automobiles braked, then honked. A red bus halted, disgorging passengers who joined a mob pressing forward. Two blue-coated policemen forced their way through, using clubs to clear a path.

"What is the matter?" I asked of a businessman on the edge of the crowd.

He shrugged. "It is only two automobile drivers in an argument. This is Ramadan, you know. We have many arguments late in the day during Ramadan."

It is also the time of the day when violent crimes are apt to be the most serious, such as someone shooting his mother-in-law or settling a family quarrel with a knife. Usually these are crimes of passion, often unplanned, the result of frayed tempers after being without food or water since dawn. Major crime rates vary between countries and areas in the Middle East. But where Islamic tradition is strong, there usually is respect for authority and crime rates are low.

"I would rather travel alone across Saudi Arabia than go

through New York's Central Park alone at night," one Aramco [Arabian American Oil Company] oil engineer said in Dhahran, Saudi Arabia. He has been mugged in New York on his last home leave. When he lost a pocketbook in Dammam, Saudi Arabia, someone turned it in to the local police station. A telephone call from the officer on duty informed him that the pocketbook, with money intact, was available any time he wanted to call for it. No hurry, though. It still would be waiting for him when he showed up, he was assured.

"Islam preaches the One God, Allah, the creator of heaven and hell, the ultimate governor of the universe," said Elie A. Salem, a slender, intense political science professor at American University of Beirut. I had met him and several other AUB professors for lunch at the Alumnae Club of the university, adjacent to the school's new $20 million medical center. Salem, a passionately involved man in anything he does, wanted to make sure that I understood the Arab and his drives.

I knew the background of Mohammed, how he preached his monotheism in a pagan Arabia, how he ranted against "graven images," how he was forced to flee from Mecca to Medina in A.D. 622 and how he returned in triumph.

"You know, of course, that the Moslem calendar dates from that flight, or what we call the Hegira," Salem explained. I knew this too, but he is a man whose enthusiasm flows right over conversational barriers. And I did enjoy listening to him. He illustrated how quickly an Arab can slide into a theological discussion, even in a luncheon meeting planned for another purpose.

I could not imagine a group of Christian political science professors slipping into a discussion about Jesus Christ over lunch. Here in Beirut, it seemed natural. Salem emphasized that three forces govern attitudes and actions of Arabs: their belief in Islam, the Arabic language, and Arabic culture.

"You must understand our religion," he said. "Islam provided Mohammed with the ideology and the movement to unify the tribes of Arabia, to make a nation out of them."

Few religions blossomed as fast as did the religion of Mohammed. It took centuries for Christianity to spread through the Roman world and into those mysterious, long-forgotten kingdoms of the East where Nestor Christians spread the gospel. In a century, Islam nearly conquered the entire world.

One of the first cities conquered was Damascus [Syria], the city visited by Mohammed as a young boy with an uncle's camel caravan. The city is cradled in an oasis created by a river that sweeps down from the mountains to the west, only to disappear in the desert sands to the east. Minarets of mosques rise on wide squares where truck traffic outweighs the automobile. Dusty trees line boulevards that lead to the walled old city in the community's heart. In that old city are miles of narrow, winding streets, lined with bazaars always crowded with people.

This is the city where Saint Paul was converted, where he had to escape over the wall as Roman soldiers sought his life. It was the home of the Omayyad dynasty, which represented that first flowering of Arab culture less than a century after Mohammed's passing. It was near the Omayyad Mosque, with its arched colonnades, that I felt the depth of Islam's hold over the people.

I had been wandering in the maze of narrow streets in [the open-air marketplace called] the souk looking for Saladin's Tomb. A tunnel from one street led past a jewelry shop. I turned into it, felt my way in semidarkness into a tiny court. Sunlight lit the small square where twenty or so boys sat on palm mats before an old mullah [religious teacher]. All sat cross-legged, the turbaned holy man holding a copy of the Koran. Shaven-headed youngsters listened, faces eager, eyes intent on lips of the gray-bearded patriarch as he read a verse from the Koran.

Then, in sing-song style they repeated the verse. Discipline was so strong that boys held their seats even after sighting me. The old mullah turned, nodded with a smile. Then, he resumed the lesson.

These boys would know the Koran by heart before they reached their teens. Their education would be based upon it, and its laws would become a part of them, to leave them with a sense of guilt should they fall away from the rules of Mohammed in later life. I knew some of those verses myself, though not in their original archaic classic Arabic.

Lo! Those who devour the wealth of orphans wrongfully, they do but swallow fire into their bellies, and they will be exposed to burning flame.

And if the debtor is in straitened circumstances, then let there be postponement to his payments; and that ye remit the debt as almsgiving would be better for you if ye did but know.

Man can have nothing but what he strives for.

Such were the substances of Mohammed's sermons in marketplaces and street corners as he converted the pagans of Arabia to Islam.

In old Jerusalem I once asked an Arab friend why the city was holy to Moslems. I knew that Islam recognizes Abraham, Moses, and other Old Testament prophets, and includes Jesus Christ as a prophet too. But why, I asked, was Jerusalem such a holy city along with Mecca and Medina for Moslems?

We were in the parking lot of the Inter-Continental Hotel on the Mount of the Ascension. Morning sunshine glinted on the golden Dome of the Rock Mosque below us, while the limestone walls which encircled the old city were just beginning to lose their early-morning pink. Behind us the Judean Hills fell away to misty distance over the Dead Sea.

"Mohammed ascended into heaven from the rock which is now covered by that dome," my friend pointed to the mosque below us.

Later that morning we drove down the steep road to the town and my friend served as a guide when we visited the spot. The story is that one night, while sleeping in Mecca, Mohammed was called to Jerusalem by the angel Gabriel. There he found a white horse awaiting him. On it, he was carried into heaven to meet all of the preceding prophets.

Mount Moriah, site of the mosque, is also reputed to be the place where Abraham started to sacrifice his son Isaac, when God bade him desist. The bare white limestone of the original mount has been left exposed within the mosque. With shoes removed, I followed our guide into a grotto within the rock.

"When Mohammed was in heaven, he told Moses that he was establishing a rule that every Moslem should pray fifty times a day toward Jerusalem," my Arab friend whispered to me. "Moses was practical. He said that wouldn't work because nobody would pray that much. He said five times a day would be enough, and that is what Mohammed decreed."

Moslems did pray when facing Jerusalem in the early days of the religion. Then, Mohammed reported that another revelation called for them to face Mecca instead.

We departed from the Harem esh Sharif (Noble Enclosure) of the mosque via the portal overlooking the Wailing Wall. Several dozen Jews prayed facing the wall, which forms one side of the foundation of the Harem esh Sharif. My Arab friend fell silent as he walked around the space that has been cleared before the Wailing Wall. I said nothing either. I have friends among Israelis and among Arabs. I can understand the feelings of both in the Israeli-Arab confrontation.

On one of several trips to the Red Sea port [of Jidda], we took Middle East Airlines [MEA] from Beirut. When boarding the Boeing 707 I noticed that one of the attractive stewardesses was fingering some worry beads, the *misbaha*. I asked to see them.

"Certainly, sir. You may keep them." She handed me a string of amber beads resembling a Catholic rosary without the cross.

I remembered something I had been told. Don't ever admire an article in Arab lands or the host might give it to you. Now I felt embarrassed, for I had merely wanted to have a look at a pair of these beads that one sees everywhere in the Middle East. Businessmen, shopkeepers, taxi drivers, everyone seems to have his *misbaha,* and I never had been told about their relationship to Islam.

"I can't keep them," I protested.

"You must," she said. Then she reassured me. "We are giving a set away to everyone on this plane."

I knew Sheik Najib Alamuddin, the American University of Beirut graduate who has built MEA into one of the best small airlines in the world. It is the sort of promotional gimmick he might have suggested.

Now that I had the string of beads, I didn't know what to do with it. My seatmate turned, smiled at me, and reached into a pocket. He took out a string of well-worn ebony beads, played with them in his fingers.

"That's all you do with them. Just that." He clicked the beads, ran them through his fingers. "See. It keeps your fingers occupied, steadies your nerves."

"Is that all?" I asked.

"That's all." He took this as a huge joke. "Many of us in this part of the world would be lost without a *misbaha.*"

"Then it's sort of like reaching for a cigaret."

"Yes," he said. "Many Moslems don't smoke, and, of course, we aren't supposed to drink alcoholic beverages. The *misbaha* is a relaxer."

A pacifier, if you will. I did discover later, though, that the *misbaha* originally came from India. The Sufi sect of Moslemism adopted it to help recall the names of Allah, such as "The Merciful," "The Compassionate," "The Patient," "The Wise," "The Venerable," "The Giver of Life," "The Giver of Death," and so on.

For most Moslems, however, it has no religious significance. Catholics started using the rosary in the thirteenth century after Franks came into contact with Moslems during the Crusades. Since Moslems had been using the *mis-baha* for four centuries at that time, the idea of the Catholic rosary may have come from Islam.

The Moslem calendar is one invention that was not adopted by the Western world. The year A.D. 622 was established as the beginning of the Moslem era after Mohammed's death. The Gregorian year of 1973, for example, is 1393 A.H. (After Hegira).

You cannot simply subtract 622 from the Gregorian calendar to find the Moslem year, because the Moslem year has 354 days, with 11 years of every 30 being leap years of 355 days each. The Islamic calendar is based on the lunar rather than the solar year. The 12 months of the year are each 29½ days. Thus, 100 Islamic years are equal to 97 Gregorian ones.

Since Arabic years are shorter than the Gregorian, the months are not tied to seasons. The first day of the new year comes earlier and earlier each year by reckoning on the Gregorian calendar. The Moslem year of 1387 started on April 11, 1967, of the Gregorian calendar. The year 1393 started on February 6, 1973.

A Moslem holy day such as the Feast of the Sacrifice, *Id-al-Adha,* will, over a period of centuries, fall on every day of the Gregorian year. It is as if Christmas and other Gregorian holidays floated, coming in winter, spring, summer, and fall, according to the day that opened each new year.

This is much less complicated to the Moslem than it may sound to the non-Moslem.

In 1973, the holy days fell in January, a cool month in Jidda and Mecca.

"When the *Hajj* is in summer—" Abbas Sindi, the [Saudi Arabian] Ministry of Information executive who became our adviser, guide, confidant, and *mutawwif* (pilgrim's guide) at Jidda, did not finish his sentence. But he shook his head. We knew that temperatures rise above one hundred degrees Fahrenheit with high humidity.

"So you roast," I said.

He nodded.

We were sitting in the lounge of the Jidda Palace Hotel in the heart of the port city. The first rain in two years was under way, a torrential downpour. Since Jidda's streets have no drainage, water flooded the streets. A driveway of the hotel became a creek with the water threatening to flow into the lounge. As we sipped mint tea, porters were rolling up the carpets to save them in case the help couldn't contain the water.

Sindi relaxes easily. He thought this was as good a place as any for him to be. With a sweep of his white robes, he sat down and called for tea, pleasant and unruffled, looking a bit like Groucho Marx masquerading as an Arab. He really could not be our *mutawwif;* as non-Moslems we could not make the *Hajj*. But he saw my interest in Islam, and he needed little encouragement to talk religion as the rain poured down outside. Arabs are poor propagandists when they seek to sell their political slogans in the West. They are supermissionaries when describing their religion to any visiting foreigners.

"I come from Mecca. Islam is part of me, like my own flesh," said he. Then, he smiled wryly. "But during the *Hajj* everyone in the Information Ministry is working nearly twenty-four hours a day, and the work starts several weeks before *Hajj* and continues several weeks after."

Making the pilgrimage is one of the five major obligations of the devout Moslem. Obligations are:

To accept belief in one God, with Mohammed as his prophet.
To pray five times a day, facing Mecca.
To give alms to the poor.
To keep the fast of Ramadan.
To make the pilgrimage to Mecca.

Obviously, every one of the 500 million Moslems cannot make the pilgrimage, perhaps because of incapacity, finances, or other personal reasons. But the *intention* must be there.

"You know also that the devout Moslem does not drink alcohol," Sindi said. He stirred the mint tea with a spoon, then added several more spoons of sugar. Highly sugared tea is the pick-me-up drink in most of the Moslem world. But most of the Moslem states do permit bars to operate for benefit of the non-Moslems, and for any fallen-away-Moslems. Saudi Arabia is tightly prohibitionist.

"How many wives do you have?" I asked Sindi. This is a question that the average Westerner seems to ask everytime he gets acquainted with a Moslem. The average Moslem regards the question with amusement. He relishes being viewed as a stud able to service several wives and concubines.

"One is enough," said Sindi. "Americans have the wrong idea about marriages in Islam. Wives are expensive. Not many men have more than one."

Polygamy, of course, has been practiced in many societies. In the hard environment of old Arabia, polygamy propagated the race and was practiced since early times. Moreover, Mohammed favored the ladies. At twenty-five he married a rich widow, Khadija, who had inherited a caravan business. Subsequently, he took other wives and fathered a huge brood. His ideas of marriage became established as law in Islam. This doesn't mean that it is compulsory to have, or that every Moslem wants, more than one wife.

Islam early split into several branches as did Christianity. Two key groups are the Sunnis and the Shiites, of which the former is much larger, some say 90 percent of all Moslems. The Shiites or Shias are found mainly in Iraq and Iran. There are also several other splinter groups, such as the Ismailis and the Druses. Within groups there are movements, usually of a reform nature, such as the Wahabis of Saudi Arabia.

Once, during the *Hajj*, we took the road to Mecca in a Chevrolet Impala with Sindi and a devout driver who was perplexed at our presence. Traffic held speed to a slow crawl. Tens of thousands of pilgrims in white robes sat in seats of taxis or limousines, or on bales of merchandise on back ends of trucks. One youth zoomed by on a motorcycle, robes flying in the wind.

A few miles from Mecca a military post bars the way. Passports are checked and no non-Moslem is allowed beyond this point. *Hajj* pilgrims will already have received their *Hajj* papers through agencies maintained in every Moslem country.

"Suppose someone pretended to be Moslem?" I asked.

Sindi shrugged. "It would not be pleasant for an imposter."

As we returned to Jidda, I noted a huge sign of painted white boulders set on a hill to form a neat Arabic script. Surely, I thought, this must be a religious inscription so located on the edge of Islam's most holy ground.

"What does that sign say?" I asked Sindi, ready to hear sacred words, perhaps from the Hadith, Mohammed's book of sayings.

Sindi squinted in the sun. "Oh, that. It says, 'Use Omo Soap.'"

The Arabic language has shaped minds ever since the time of Mohammed. It should not be surprising to find it in advertising.

When Mohammed's revelations were collected by his successors into the Koran, this became the first book in Arabic. Writers of the seventh century used the refined speech of the day, and their interpretation became accepted as authentic grammar for classic Arabic. Because the Koran was revealed in it, it became a holy language, too sacred to change, a polished, stylized idiom far removed from the colloquialisms of the street.

All languages govern cultures, shape forces within society. Some languages are more powerful than others and Arabic is a strong one. Roman Catholicism early adopted Latin and it became a binding force in the Church. English has become the lingua franca of world business, pop culture, and science. It carries Anglo-Saxon culture everywhere, much to the annoyance of the French, who feel that the world would be better off with French.

Linguistic eloquence became a virtue in Islam. In the eighth and ninth centuries, when Arabs had conquered half the known world, their language was the binding force for welding empires together. It served first as the medium for absorbing cultures of Greek and Persian predecessors. Then Arabs used their classic Arabic to transform those cultures into something of their own, a truly Islamic culture.

Today [in 1974], when Arabs boast of the glory of past civilizations, they usually mean that period during the rule of the Omayyad dynasty in Damascus and its successor, the Abbasid dynasty in Baghdad, when Arabs excelled in medicine, optics, astronomy, mathematics, and other sciences. Books of savants were written in Arabic and translated into Latin to become text books in Europe. Arab knowledge helped preserve culture when Europe was in its Dark Ages. Al-Baladhuri's *History of the Conquests* furthered the study of history as an intellectual pursuit. Rhazes, a great Arab physician, performed pioneer research in smallpox, detailing finds in a report written with penetrating clarity. The science of algebra was developed.

That glorious era ended with internal bickering. This was followed by invasions of Mongol hordes, Turkish conquests, intervention by Western powers, and Arab subservience.

In the nineteenth and early twentieth centuries Western powers dictated events in the Middle East. In Iraq when a guest overstays his leave, the Iraqi says, "He stays like the British." Britain occupied Egypt in 1882 for what it termed a "temporary" period, and troops were not withdrawn until 1952. When France won certain rights to represent Catholics in the Middle East from a corrupt Turkish ruler, it transformed that "right" into a political weapon for colonializing parts of the Arab world. Russia continually sought a route to a warm-water port in the south through the Middle East. Britain barred any such move by Russia.

The rivalry of Western powers existed into the oil age of the twentieth century. It provided a background for the first discovery of oil in the Middle East, a discovery that was finally to provide Middle Easterners with the strength they had lacked for centuries.

II. DIVISIONS AMONG THE ARAB NATIONS

EDITOR'S INTRODUCTION

Although the peoples of the Arab countries have much ·in common—their primary language being Arabic and their chief religion Islam—the Arab world has long been known for its bitter divisions and seemingly irreconcilable disputes. The stern fundamentalist leader of Libya is at odds with his less austere coreligionists in other countries. Not long ago, Jordan fought a war of extermination against Arab guerrilla groups located within its boundaries. Syria and Egypt have been quarreling for years. So have Iran and Iraq. Lebanon has endured a deadly civil war between Christians and Moslems, with different Moslem factions at times fighting one another. The struggle has virtually destroyed Lebanon's political and social structure and has severely disrupted its economic life.

This section presents articles illustrating aspects of the division in the Arab world today. The first article deals with Lebanon, recounting the background of the fighting and the details of the truce that, it is hoped, will bring peace to the ravaged land. Since the spring of 1975 twenty-two separate cease-fires have been arranged—and each has broken down in new and savage rounds of fighting. In one grim December weekend, for example, more than 100 people were killed and 200 kidnapped. It is estimated that the fighting has killed 10,000 people and wounded at least 25,000 in the last ten months of 1975. For a nation of under 3 million, these are staggering figures.

The next article, from the New York *Times,* offers a brief sketch of the views of Colonel Muammar al-Qaddafi of Libya who has proclaimed his support for revolutionary causes in all parts of the world and has backed his statements with generous supplies of money and weapons to guerrilla organizations. The final article in this section looks at the Persian Gulf area where the jockeying for power among the nations of the region has resulted in a buildup of arms.

LEBANON: PEACE OR TRUCE? [1]

In the millennia since the days of the Phoenicians, the place we . . . call Lebanon has been, by virtue of its location, a regional center for trade, commerce and finance, and a haven for weaker peoples fleeing from the strong.

It survived, and thrived, not because of its own strength, but because the stronger people around it felt the need for the function it fulfilled.

Now [in early February 1976], after 10 months of civil war that left 10,000 of its 2.6 million people dead and cost its economy an estimated total of $8 billion, that Lebanon is no more.

The country itself is intact, and the people have begun to dig out from under the debris in this, the third week of an uneasy truce between the factions of right-wing Christians and left-wing Moslems and Palestinians, a truce dictated by neighboring Syria with the blessing of the United States and the Soviet Union, and the tacit acquiescence of Israel.

As reports come in of the regrouping and rearming of the combatants, there is no certainty that this truce will hold, though it is given a better chance than its twenty-two predecessors. Even if it does—and the complex motives for the fighting are far from resolved—the consensus is that Lebanon will never be the same again.

The precarious political and social equilibrium of the country, built on a forty-four-year-old illusion (the 1932 census, Lebanon's last) and the political "gentlemen's agreement" based upon it, is shattered.

[1] Article by Michael J. Berlin, staff writer. New York *Post*. p 21. F. 7, '76. Reprinted by permission of New York *Post*. © 1976, New York Post Corporation.

And so is the Lebanese economy. Many of the banks are gone; the regional offices of global corporations have sought safer havens; trade patterns are disrupted, and the old free-wheeling capitalist system is endangered because the social compact upon which it was based is no more, and a new one remains to be painfully constructed.

The Lebanon, as the country long was called, had been the trading fulcrum of the Mediterranean world since the Phoenician coastal towns of Tyre and Sidon built their ships from the forests of its inland mountain range. Famous everywhere were the cedars of Lebanon. It emerged from the Turkish empire into the twentieth century with seventeen officially recognized religious sects sharing power in a rigidly structured but haphazardly run political system.

The first of these sects to arrive was the Maronite Christians, fleeing from orthodox Byzantine Christianity in the sixth century. Five centuries later, Islamic heretics—the Druze—arrived.

The Turks took over in the sixteenth century, and during a Druze-Maronite civil war in 1860, France intervened on behalf of her fellow Christians to force the creation of an autonomous Turkish "sanjak" or province of Lebanon, with a Christian majority and a Christian governor, in the southern half of what is now Lebanon.

When the French took over both Syria and Lebanon from Turkey after World War I, they enlarged Lebanon by combining the Christian south with the Moslem north, which had been part of Syria under the Turks.

"Gentlemen's Agreement"

Lebanon became independent in 1943 (though French occupation troops did not leave until 1946). The complex unwritten agreement, based on the 1932 census showing a small Christian majority, guaranteed the Maronites and, to a lesser extent, the Sunni Moslem sect, political dominance.

The president and the army commander were Christians, and the parliament was apportioned according to a 6-to-5

Christian-Moslem ratio. The . . . [premier] (appointed by the president) was a Sunni, the speaker of the house a . . . [Shiite] Moslem.

This division was originally intended to be temporary until the Lebanese achieved a sense of national identity, which would then allow the Christian Arabs to lose their fear of being swallowed up by their surrounding Moslem neighbors.

Over the years, however, circumstances increased rather than decreased the Christian sense of insecurity. Towns, schools and social strata emphasized the fragmentation. The Moslem population grew faster, and now constitutes an estimated 60 percent of the nation. The surrounding Arab world was swept by pan-Arab and Islamic nationalism, which reinforced the Christian sense of isolation. Other minorities—Armenians and Kurds from Turkey and Iraq—flocked to Lebanon, accentuating differences. The Palestinian refugees (some 300,000 now) entered Lebanon, and their growing autonomy threatened the sovereignty of the Lebanese state.

As a result, the Christian community saw its survival in continued control of the political system, and in maintaining the outdated 1943 compact against reform.

With that political control came social stratification, as the Maronites and the Sunni Moslem establishment evolved into the wealthy classes. The . . . [Shiite] Moslems—the largest (and poorest) single grouping in Lebanon today—perceived that their own interest lay in the diverse forces marshaled against the establishment: pan-Arabism, Islamization, secularization (to break the system of proportion by religious sects) and socialism (to break the economic and class structures).

The radicalization of the have-not Moslem and Druze groups was stimulated by the parallel radicalization of the Palestinians in Lebanon, the availability of educational opportunity, and the failure of the establishment to correct the disparities between the very poor and the very rich.

It was also fostered by the presence in Lebanon of political influences from every Arab nation, from the Iraqis on the left to the Libyans on the right. Among the outside Arab influences, the Syrian was the most potent, for the Syrians, regardless of ideology, still regard Lebanon as part of "Greater Syria," to be reclaimed at some future time. They have, for example, always refused to exchange ambassadors with Lebanon, for this reason.

The system underwent its first test in 1958, when the tide of pan-Arabism swept the area, uniting Syria and Egypt briefly, toppling the pro-Western monarchy in Iraq, causing the United States to conclude that there was a Soviet plot to take over the area, and impelling Lebanon's pro-Western Christian President Camille Chamoun to refuse to step down after his first six-year term.

This confluence of events produced a Lebanese civil war —minor by comparison with 1975—the landing of fifteen thousand American Marines in Lebanon and of British troops in Jordan, to protect Western clients.

American backing went to the most anti-Communist of the Lebanese factions, the Christian Phalangists of Pierre Gemayel, in 1958, while a rival Christian chieftain, Suleiman Franjieh, then allied with Sunni Moslem leader Rashid Karami, was granted temporary asylum in Syria by a young officer named Hafez Assad.

Now Assad is president of Syria, Franjieh is president of Lebanon, Karami is . . . [premier] of Lebanon, at odds with Franjieh, and Chamoun is in Karami's cabinet, but still allied with Gemayel and the Christian right wing.

Rise of the Palestinians

Lebanon prospered after that 1958 flare-up, staying out of the 1957 Arab-Israeli war, until the rise of the Palestinian guerrilla groupings after 1967.

The guerrilla groups took control of the refugee camps, then the southern area bordering Israel, and when the Israelis retaliated against Lebanese territory in the wake of terrorist raids across the border, anti-Palestinian sentiment was aroused in the Christian-dominated twelve-thousand-man Lebanese army and within the right-wing Christian groups.

In a 1969 confrontation between the army and the Palestinians, Syria sent Palestinian detachments under its control to help the guerrillas. Another confrontation in 1973 resulted in a closing of the Syria-Lebanon border for three months. The result was an agreement with the Palestinian Liberation Organization [PLO], accepting the theory of Lebanese sovereignty, but preserving the reality of Palestinian freedom of operation and armed control of its bases.

Christians, stopped by gun-toting Palestinians at roadblocks, began to fear that their control of Lebanon was being eaten away. Moderate proposals from the Moslem political left for reform of the system—easing the strict proportional allotment of jobs on the lower levels of the civil service, for example, and a greater Moslem role in the army—were perceived as threats.

The Palestinians saw the left-wing Moslem groups as natural allies against the Christians who wished to limit Palestinian freedom of movement, and proceeded to arm the Lebanese leftist groups. Massive inflation hit the poorer levels of Lebanese society in 1973 and 1974, and workers rioted in the major cities.

The Libyans, intent on the Islamization of Lebanon, provided some $30 million to $40 million to help arm the Moslem factions.

The tinder was dry and ready, and the spark was struck in a Christian suburb of the capital, Beirut, on April 13, 1975. The Phalangists had gathered for the ceremonial opening of a Maronite church, and one was killed by shots from a passing car. Later that day, the Phalangists stopped a bus filled with Palestinians in the same neighborhood, and killed 26 of them. Four days of fighting followed, leaving 150 dead.

Government Begins to Falter

The government . . . of [Premier] Rashid Solh fell as a result of its failure to act in the crisis, Phalangist-Palestinian fighting flared again, and after a three-day attempt by President Franjieh to form a military government, he was forced to designate Karami as . . . [premier]—a man who had held the office eight times before, and still held the respect of most establishment Christian and Moslem factions.

But although Karami formed a six-man cabinet, it excluded both extremes, and it became clear that neither he nor Franjieh could control their radical elements.

There was heavy fighting in Beirut in early July, and isolated incidents for the rest of the summer. The real fighting began in September, with battles between the Moslem city of Tripoli (Karami's district) and the neighboring Christian hill town of Zgharta (Franjieh's own base), in the north.

The fighting spread to Beirut, this time almost exclusively between the Lebanese factions, with the same Palestinians helping the leftists, and Yasir Arafat of the PLO trying to mediate, along with the Syrians.

It was not until the end of October that the Beirut fighting really hit the wealthy sections, causing an exodus of foreign residents and ending all semblances of government and economic activity in Lebanon. Unlike 1958, the United States announced publicly at this point that it would not intervene.

There were numerous attempts at mediation—by the Vatican, which otherwise remained silent about the situation of Lebanon's Christian community, by former French Foreign Minister Couve de Murville, and several times by Arafat and the Syrians.

The Phalangists began to call for a partition of Lebanon, but Syria warned in November that it would use force to prevent it. In December, the truces and battles continued to follow one another, and even during lulls there was incessant sniper fire, kidnappings and taking of hostages on both sides. Arms flowed to the Christians from Western Europe, and to the Moslems from Syria, as the Moslems accused the United States, Israel, Jordan and Iran of financing the Christians, and the Christians claimed the Moslem money was coming from Iraq, Syria, Libya and the PLO.

The Soviet Union apparently backed the Moslem military action, for the Lebanese Communist party, which Moscow controls, was engaged in the heavy fighting.

The United States shifted its backing away from the Christian militants and the inactive Franjieh to the peace-making attempts of Karami, with overt gestures of support, and private encouragement from US Ambassador G. McMurtries Godley, whose bulletproof limousine often served as the only rescue vehicle able and willing to evacuate American citizens caught in crossfires in their hotels.

The Israelis maintained that Syria and the PLO were encouraging the radical elements in the fighting, but Western Arabists in Beirut, including the Americans, contended that Syria's interest lay in ending the bloodshed and gradually increasing its influence in Lebanon by political rather than military means.

The fighting came to a head in mid-January [1976], when the Palestinians actively entered the fighting at the side of the Lebanese Moslem leftists, and the Lebanese army, which had been inactive except for brief mediating roles, flew two air sorties against a Palestinian column besieging a Christian town—in violation of Karami's instructions.

The Phalangists laid siege to two Palestinian camps astride key road junctions, and at that point the Syrians sent in three thousand troops of the Palestine Liberation Army—based in and controlled by Syria rather than Arafat—to turn the tide of battle of January 18.

Two days later the last Christian prospect vanished when Israel, bending to stiff American pressure, announced it would not enter the fighting unless regular Syrian army units crossed the Lebanese border. Syria didn't have to.

The Lebanese army still didn't move on behalf of the Christians (apparently, it didn't trust its Moslem rank and file to obey such orders), and on January 22, the Syrian truce was declared, combined with an agreement to reform the Lebanese political system.

The reforms include equal distribution of parliamentary seats between Moslems and Christians, increasing the power of the [Sunni] Moslem . . . [premier] to equal that of the [Maronite] Christian president, selection of the . . . [premier] by parliament, rather than the president, and (for the Christians), another uncertain promise that the PLO will live up to its previous commitments to respect Lebanese sovereignty. [Other provisions of the truce include the continuation of the tradition that the speaker of the house be a Shiite Moslem, and a ban on the apportionment of civil service positions among the country's religious communities, except for those positions named in this paragraph.—Ed.]

Future Questions

A US Commerce Department analyst, Norman Howard, writing in the periodical *Current History* . . . [in January 1976], sums up the situation this way:

It seems clear that Lebanon can never be the same again. The killing and destruction have probably been too great to allow a return to the old relationships [between the religious sects] and haphazard manner of running the country.

Major political reform may have to await the next parliamentary and presidential elections, scheduled for April and August, 1976, respectively, but there must be reform if the country is to survive as a democratic state—or even to survive at all.

[In mid-March 1976 the Syrian-dictated truce broke down amid new Christian-Moslem street fighting, mass desertions from the Lebanese army, and an attempt by a group of army officers to seize power and oust President Franjieh.—Ed.]

QADDAFI: BACKER OF REVOLUTIONS [2]

One major reason the fighting in Lebanon has resulted in so many deaths is that the weapons being used are mod-

[2] From "Qaddafi of Libya Believes in Backing Almost Any Revolution." *New York Times.* p E 2. N. 2, '75. © 1975 by The New York Times Company. Reprinted by permission.

ern and efficient. They are also expensive and, though details are impossible to prove, diplomatic sources in Beirut say that in . . . [1975] the Libyan government of Colonel Muammar al-Qaddafi has spent more than $30 million financing leftist Moslem factions in their fight against rightwing Christians. The Christian groups apparently rely on their own affluent supporters for arms financing.

The Libyan leader publicly proclaims his support for both Arab and non-Arab revolutionaries. Some of the $8 billion in annual Libyan oil revenue has financed revolutionaries not only in Lebanon but across the world from the Arabian peninsula to the Philippines.

At one time or another, rebels from Dhofar in the Sultanate of Oman, secessionists from Eritrea in northern Ethiopia, black nationalists in the United States, the Irish Republican Army and the Japanese Red Army have turned to the colonel for assistance. More often than not, they get it.

The biggest contributions have gone to the Palestinian organizations engaged in the fight against Israel. In a speech in his capital, Tripoli, . . . Colonel Qaddafi offered to help every Palestinian or Arab who joined that fight. But he added: "Henceforth I intend to fight the United States and Britain on their own grounds, and in their own backyards."

At the time, representatives of the American Black Panthers and the Irish Republican Army were in Tripoli and Colonel Qaddafi confirmed he would help them.

The colonel's antagonism toward Britain goes back to 1972, when he encouraged Malta's break with Britain and offered Premier Dom Mintoff financial assistance if he would discontinue giving facilities on the island to North Atlantic Treaty Organization fleets. That same year, Libyan air force planes tried to transport weapons to Uganda to help President Idi Amin against troops that were said to have invaded the country from neighboring Tanzania. However, the planes were intercepted over Sudan and turned back.

On the surface, the Libyan policy appears to be contradictory in that Colonel Qaddafi is helping the Catholics in

Ireland, and the Moslems of the Philippines who are fighting the predominantly Christian regime of President Ferdi-
nand E. Marcos. But the Libyan leader, who sees his role as
continuing the revolutionary mission started by the late
[Egyptian] President Gamal Abdel Nasser, has his own
philosophy of revolution.

He advocates action within three circles: the Arab circle,
the Islamic circle, and the international circle.

Attaining Arab unity and keeping up the struggle against
Israel are the main components of Libya's pan-Arab policy.
Within this framework Colonel Qaddafi tried unsuccessfully
to merge Libya first with Egypt and later with Tunisia. His
aid to the Palestinian guerrilla movement and to its international allies, such as the Japanese Red Army, falls within
this objective as well.

Islamic consciousness always ran deep in the Libyan revolution that brought Colonel Qaddafi to power in 1969, when
he and his junta of young army officers overthrew aging
King Idris. This explains the aid given to Moslem rebels in
the Philippines, and Eritrea.

In the international circle, the Libyan revolution in-
veighs against "world imperialism." The United States and
Britain have been identified by the colonel as its leaders.

The Flirtation With Moscow

Ideologically opposed to communism, Colonel Qaddafi
in the past lumped the Soviet Union with the other impe-
rialist powers. His attitude, however, began to change following his falling-out with President Anwar Sadat of Egypt
. . . [in 1973].

Objecting strongly to Mr. Sadat's policy of securing peace
with Israel, and already dismayed because Egypt had
spurned his offers of unity, the Libyan leader turned to
Moscow. Earlier . . . [in 1975] Libya bought $800 million
worth of Soviet weapons.

Colonel Qaddafi has established strong links to the Marx-
ists inside the Palestinian movement led by Dr. George

Habash, the secretary general of the Popular Front for the Liberation of Palestine. Press reports have said Libya has allocated $16 million to these guerrilla groups.

But . . . [during 1975], the campaign against the Egyptian regime has dominated Colonel Qaddafi's foreign policy, prompting President Sadat to suggest that the volatile Libyan leader was "sick in the head."

Western diplomats believe the Libyan revolutionary drive has reached its peak and expect it to recede for three main reasons:

First, a drop in oil revenue resulting from a sharp decrease in world demand for petroleum; second, the failure so far of Colonel Qaddafi's endeavors to unite his country with other Arab states; third, a split has developed inside the eleven-man Revolutionary Council, which rules Libya.

One member of the council, Major Omar Meheishi, defected to Tunisia in August [1975] amid speculation that he had tried but failed to overthrow Colonel Qaddafi. In a later speech, Colonel Qaddafi indirectly substantiated speculation about the affair when he spoke harshly of "the coup makers" in Libya.

PERSIAN GULF RIVALRIES [3]

Reprinted from *U.S. News & World Report*.

A wide-ranging struggle for influence in the Persian Gulf is turning that oil-rich region into a dangerous new arena of rivalry between the United States and Russia.

The dizzying arms race that is under way has seen the gulf states triple their military spending . . . [since 1972]. More than $6 billion was spent in 1974 alone, according to the London-based International Institute for Strategic Studies.

The United States—as well as Britain and France—is selling Iran, Saudi Arabia and the smaller sheikdoms the most

[3] From "Persian Gulf: Where Big Powers Are Playing a Risky Game." *U.S. News & World Report*. 78:49-50+. Mr. 10, '75.

sophisticated weapons available. The Russians are pouring
arms into Iraq and South Yemen.

At stake: dominance over a region that supplies at least
40 percent of the oil consumed daily by non-Communist
countries. Every fifteen minutes, a tanker filled with oil sails
through the Strait of Hormuz at the head of the gulf en
route to refineries around the world.

Competition between the United States and Russia in the
Persian Gulf is complicated by rivalries on two other levels.

Among Iran, Saudi Arabia and Iraq, each of which is
resolved to emerge as the region's number one power, and
between the conservative sheikdoms and leftist Arab forces
who want to impose "progressive" rule. Says one expert on
the Middle East:

"In the gulf . . . [in 1975], there are almost as many
separate interests and conflicts as there are states. The big
question is, who will impose peace on the region, Iran, Iraq
or Saudi Arabia? Or will one or both of the superpowers
intervene?"

Roots of . . . tension in the Persian Gulf go back to
Britain's decision in mid-1971 to withdraw its forces from
the Trucial States—now called the United Arab Emirates—
made up of Dubai, Abu Dhabi, Sharjah and four smaller
states.

Ever since, one power after another has tried to step into
the vacuum left by the British departure, attracted by the
gulf's enormous oil reserves and aware that the region's economic and political backwardness makes it an easy target
for unrest and revolution.

Enter the Shah

Latest contender for supremacy is Iran, whose Shah Mohammed Reza Pahlevi dreams of reviving the power of the
ancient Persian empire and controlling the entrance to the
Persian Gulf. The shah has both the money and the manpower to realize his ambitions. Not only is Iran the world's

fourth-largest oil producer, but its 32 million people make it the most populous nation on the Persian Gulf.

In his determination to build the Iranian military force into one of the most powerful in the world, the shah has been purchasing American weapons with little regard for the cost.

Since 1971, the shah has increased the number of combat planes in his air force by more than 50 percent—to 216 craft. . . .

Iran has the world's largest fleet of military hovercraft—used to patrol the Persian Gulf—and soon will become the third-largest owner of helicopters, behind the United States and Russia. Retired US Army aviators, working for a private American firm, are training Iranian pilots in the techniques of combat-helicopter assaults developed by the United States in the Vietnam war.

Other items either delivered or on order from America include an air defense network, antitank missiles, air-to-ground and surface-to-air missiles and a half-dozen of the latest guided-missile destroyers. The United States, which has about 700 military advisers stationed in the country—plus thousands of civilian technicians—also is helping Iran construct a multimillion-dollar port at Bandar Abbas, which guards the entrance to the Strait of Hormuz. . . .

According to Mideast authorities, the shah has two major objectives in his drive to modernize his armed forces: to make Iran the dominant power in a wide expanse of territory stretching from the Middle East into Asia and to counter Russian efforts to bring change to the Persian Gulf.

Irons in the Fire

To reach these goals, the shah has put his irons into almost every fire in the region.

☐ In Oman, gateway to the Persian Gulf, two thousand Iranian troops are fighting alongside weak Omani forces against Soviet-backed guerrillas in the southern Province of Dhofar. The Iranian air force has been given orders to protect Oman against outside attack.

☐ The shah has thrown his protective mantle over the tiny sheikdoms of the United Arab Emirates and has committed Iran to support the independence of Kuwait in the face of Iraqi claims to territory.

☐ In Iraq, itself, the shah is giving arms and military equipment to rebel Kurdish tribesmen who are seeking autonomy from the Baghdad government. Iraq claims that Iranian forces are directly involved in the bloody civil war and charges that two of its jets recently were shot down by Iranian surface-to-air missiles. [In March 1975 Iran ended this aid in order to improve relations with Iraq.—Ed.]

☐ Iran has promised massive financial aid to neighboring Afghanistan—perhaps as much as $2 billion—to enable the Kabul government to survive without becoming dependent upon the Soviet Union.

☐ The shah is supplying India with about two thirds of its petroleum—at good prices—and has invested in refineries in India. But he has warned that Moslem Iran would intervene against India if New Delhi were to launch another attack on Moslem Pakistan.

☐ Iran also is supporting both sides in the Arab-Israeli controversy—providing oil to Israel and financial aid to Egypt. The shah's . . . [1975] "tilt" toward the Arabs, according to Western experts, does not mean that Iranian forces—who are non-Arab—would join a new war against Israel. Instead, they say the move was designed to force Arab recognition of the shah's growing influence in the Middle East.

Iraq's Countermeasures

Primary target of Iran's military buildup is Iraq. But Iraq also has taken steps of its own to strengthen its armed forces—with the help of $2.4 billion in Russian aid since March, 1974.

Behind Baghdad's arms drive: Fear that Iran will block Iraq's way out of the Persian Gulf; Russia's determination to use Iraq as Moscow's alter ego in establishing Soviet authority throughout the gulf; longstanding border disputes with Iran and Kuwait, and the unresolved Kurdish rebellion.

For the moment [in 1975], it is the Kurdish war that preoccupies the shaky Socialist government in Baghdad.

The bulk of Iraq's 112,000-man armed forces is engaged in the battle against 5,000 Kurdish tribesmen who are proving difficult to defeat. Already, the Iraqis have suffered 5,000 casualties, and authorities say the war is far from over.

Iraq's radical Baath government has tried in the past to negotiate a settlement with the Kurds. Yet many authorities are convinced that enmity is too deep and Kurdish demands —including control of oil fields near Kirkuk—are too stiff to permit an early end to the fighting.

Under a new military agreement signed last December [1974], Russia supplied Iraq with a squadron of TU-22 bombers to aid in the war against the Kurds, and Russian pilots are believed flying the planes in combat. Additionally, Soviet airmen are piloting new MIG-23s, not only in Iraq itself, but on flights over the gulf sheikdoms. About three thousand Russian advisers are stationed in Iraq.

In return for massive Soviet aid, Iraq granted the Russians unlimited use of certain Iraqi ports and airfields and is expanding its harbors—including the port at Umm Qasr— for use by Moscow's Indian Ocean fleet.

Across the gulf from Iran, other Arab states also are arming themselves. They worry over possible trouble from Soviet-backed Arab leftists and fear domination by their ambitious Persian neighbor.

The Saudis' Role

Leading the way is wealthy Saudi Arabia . . . [which] sympathizes with . . . Iran's efforts to stem the flow of radical ideas in the gulf, and an uneasy partnership now exists between the two. . . .

But . . . [Saudi Arabia] is alarmed over Iran's growing military might and does not relish playing the role of junior partner to the Iranians.

To help close the military gap with Iran, Saudi Arabia . . . [in 1975] completed a $1.5 billion arms deal with the United States, including the purchase of several squadrons of F-5E fighter planes. This followed a $700 million weapons order in 1974.

With the US Defense Department serving as go-between and supplying the weapons, Saudi Arabia also has hired a private American company to train its national guard to protect the nation's oil fields from attack. GI veterans of the Vietnam war are being recruited to handle the training.

To further strengthen their armed forces, the Saudis bought $1 billion worth of arms from France in 1974, including 450 tanks and 38 Mirage fighters. Frigates and minesweepers are under order for the small navy, and production of missiles under French supervision is considered likely.

Saudi Arabia also has announced plans to construct a large military base at Hofar al Batin, strategically located close to the Iraqi border and Kuwait. With another air base at Dhahran to the south, the new installation will give the Saudi air force two effective springboards from which to cover the entire Persian Gulf region.

To the south of Saudi Arabia in poverty-stricken Oman, Soviet weapons have kept alive a rebellion that has been waged since 1965, with guerrillas striking into Dhofar Province from sanctuaries in South Yemen next door. Sultan Qabus ibn Said, a young Western-educated ruler, is battling the insurgents with the help of Iranian troops and about three hundred British officers who are leading Omani forces. Saudi Arabia and Jordan have also given assistance.

A country of only 650,000 people, Oman has earmarked 40 percent of its $600 million budget in 1975 for the war, including a sharp expansion of the Omani armed forces.

Plans call for the raising of four new regiments, doubling the size of the small navy, and purchasing the Anglo-French Jaguar aircraft which—in theory—will enable Oman to make long-range attacks on South Yemen.

Other arms deals: helicopter troop carriers and missiles from the United States, and ground-to-air missiles and radar systems from the British. Cost is no deterrent. Because it is strategically situated at the mouth of the Persian Gulf, Oman can count on unlimited support against the guerrillas from Iran as well as other anti-Communist states.

Not to be left out of the arms race, Kuwait, with a population of one million, allocated $1.5 billion for modernization of its defense forces in mid-1974. This tiny country has become the first Mideast nation to receive France's most advanced aircraft, the Mirage F-1, and has purchased Skyhawk fighters from the United States.

Although tremendously wealthy from oil, the Kuwaiti government deeply fears Iraq. With a small population—60 percent of which is made up of foreign workers, including skilled Palestinians—Kuwait would have to rely on Iran or Saudi Arabia for its defense if its border dispute with Baghdad turned into a full-scale war.

The United Arab Emirates also are involved in major arms purchases. Dubai recently purchased surface-to-air missiles and French Mirage jets, and Abu Dhabi bought a $110 million radar system from Britain.

The Emirates depend heavily on British officers and advisers to help them with internal security and commercial transactions with the outside world. But radical Arab elements are . . . calling for the expulsion of the British and for their replacement by Arabs. Western-oriented Iran and Saudi Arabia are concerned that the sheikdoms could be threatened internally if the British are forced to leave.

Copyright 1975 U.S. News & World Report, Inc.

III. THE ARABS' NEW WEALTH

EDITOR'S INTRODUCTION

The oil-producing Arab countries are being flooded with billions of dollars in revenue as a result of increased petroleum prices. Never has there been so massive a transfer of funds to one area of the world in so short a time. While it was at first feared that this shift would enable the Arabs literally to buy up large parts of the Western world, the apprehension proved to be unfounded.

However, with their new wealth, the Arab countries are funding many large-scale economic development projects which could stimulate a more rapid pace of economic growth and an improvement in the conditions of life for large numbers of people. Yet the region lacks technicians and technical know-how in some fields and still requires Western expertise. That need presents the West with a vast array of business opportunities as the stage is set for new commercial relationships between the industrialized world and the Middle East.

One such new relationship is that between the Saudi Arabian government and the Arabian American Oil Company (Aramco), the world's most important single oil enterprise. Aramco is presently owned and operated by four US oil companies. It is responsible for almost all of the oil produced by Saudi Arabia, the world's largest oil exporter. However, during the last decade the Saudi Arabian government has been purchasing Aramco's physical assets (oil wells, drilling rigs, and pipelines, for example) and leasing them back to the company for a fee. In March 1976 an agreement was reached between the four Aramco partners and the Saudi Arabian government on terms for the eventual takeover of these assets. Once the agreement takes effect, the Arabian American Oil Company will be the agent supervising the production of Saudi oil and the operation of Saudi equipment.

This section presents articles dealing with events in a number of Middle East countries under the impact of the dollar influx. The first selection is an article from *Business Week* which looks at the Middle East as a whole and describes some of the ambitious plans being implemented in a number of countries by government and business leaders. The article also speaks of the response of US and European industrial interests.

The second article examines Iran. The article focuses on the plans, methods, and objectives of the shah, who holds complete and unchallenged authority in that country. The shah has initiated many far-reaching changes in his country in the past few years. He has also made Iran the region's foremost military power, as he continues to lead the fight for higher oil prices and a Persian Gulf region devoid of any outside military presence.

The next selection discusses Egypt. Badly scarred by the series of wars with Israel and facing grave economic problems (compounded by a rapidly increasing population), Egypt has indicated its desire for a peace settlement to enable it to concentrate its energies on badly needed development efforts. As the article shows, work has begun on a wide range of important projects. What is needed is a secure and lasting Middle East peace to enable this work to continue in the years ahead.

The article that follows deals with the politics and economics of Iraq, Saudi Arabia, Kuwait, and several smaller Persian Gulf states. Iraq has faced long-term political instability and, at the same time, has contended with the armed struggle for autonomy of a determined minority group, the Kurds. Saudi Arabia, an extremely conservative monarchy, was shaken by the 1975 assassination of its king, but its political stability does not appear to have been affected. Among the major challenges facing Kuwait and the smaller states is how to invest their oil revenues wisely in order to provide a base for viable economies when the wells run dry in the not-too-distant future.

The last article in this section, by Ray Vicker of the *Wall Street Journal,* concerns a little-known country, Sudan, and describes how Arab governments are investing oil-generated revenues in its development as a potential source of food for the region.

BUILDING A NEW MIDDLE EAST [1]

Inundated by a tidal wave of oil money, the underdeveloped countries of the Middle East have suddenly become affluent—some to a remarkable degree—and they are beginning to act the part. With their plentiful petrodollars, they are building new economies almost from scratch. Surprisingly, after bouts of doctrinaire socialism in the post-World War II era, the Middle East is . . . [in 1975] one of the few places in the world where private enterprise is making a comeback. . . .

[During the 1960s] the Arab world seemed to be drifting not only into socialism but into strident nationalism and bitter anti-Americanism. . . . [In 1975], in a region whose combined gross national product nearly doubled from $50 billion in 1973 to more than $95 billion . . . [in 1974], there is a strong incentive to concentrate on attaining material goals that once were considered beyond reach. Even such militant governments as Syria's are becoming more moderate.

Affluence breeds impatience with wants deferred, so the oil-rich nations are spending as though cars, houses, hospitals, schools, and telephone systems were going out of style. Beyond such immediate needs, they are plowing their surplus into refineries, steel mills, and manufacturing plants that will provide jobs and income for the future.

Affluence is also a social broadener, and it is because of

[1] From an article in *Business Week.* p 38-44+. My. 26, '75. Reprinted from the May 26, 1975 issue of *Business Week* by special permission. © 1975 by McGraw-Hill, Inc.

this that closed societies such as Saudi Arabia's are beginning to open up under the impact of increased travel and business contacts. Reaching further afield, Arabs and Iranians are using their money to make friends and influence people with foreign aid.

Evidence of the new money is everywhere. A fleet of five hundred canary-yellow Dodges, imported by Syria . . . [in 1974] for use as taxis, now brightens the streets of Damascus. Air-conditioned shops in Jidda's [Saudi Arabia] *souk*, or bazaar, offer expensive English worsteds, and veiled women customers sniff vials that exhale, not the perfumes of Arabia, but the essences of Revlon and Chanel.

More significant for the future of the region is a massive inflow of capital equipment for industry and for expansion of the economic infrastructure. Even so, suppliers are unable to keep up with demand. . . . One problem is that the sea lanes, railroads, and highway routes to the Middle East are clogged with traffic that bulges with goods ordered by the new rich.

Out beyond the present heady flush of spending, the foresighted are planning for a more permanent source of wealth. Iran's real GNP [gross national product] jumped a phenomenal 40 percent . . . [in 1974], stoked by oil production. Oil can't be depended on to yield many more gains like that. But $69 billion in economic development spending should sustain annual growth of 14 percent to 16 percent for the next . . . [few] years at least, and create a permanent basis for healthy growth after that. [For an account of Iran's development, see "Oil, Grandeur and a Challenge to the West," in this section, below.]

Such forced-draft expansion is stirring inflation, straining manpower, and creating bottlenecks in the economy, but the Iranians have no intention of slowing down. "We are going to stretch ourselves to our limits, physically and mentally. We are going to push ahead as fast as we can," vows Mahmud Mehran, Iran's deputy minister of economy and finance.

In Saudi Arabia, with its population of only six million and its narrow economic base, the impact of a five-year, $150 billion investment plan is likely to be even more dramatic. One important issue . . . [in 1975], with far-reaching consequences for Saudi Arabia's traditional social structure, is whether to allow women to work outside the home and thus expand the country's meager labor force.

From the oil-rich nations, the boom is spilling over to neighboring countries. Egypt and Syria alone received commitments of financial help totaling more than $4 billion from their rich neighbors . . . [in 1974]—exclusive of military aid. And Arab governments have set up a flock of development funds to finance projects in less affluent countries within the region.

Petrodollars are also sifting into those countries through trade, transport services, private investment, and money sent home by workers who have gone off to jobs in the oil-rich areas. "This is the first time that shares issued by companies in Jordan have been oversubscribed," says Mamduh Abu-Hassan, chairman of Jordan Ceramics Industry, Ltd., a joint venture with a German firm in Amman.

For the United States, the roaring pace of business in the Middle East is reflected in a sharp rise in trade with the area. And despite the oil price rise, the United States is running a trade surplus with the area. What that means is that Europe and Japan, the biggest buyers of Middle East oil, are footing most of the bill for the area's prosperity. Petrodollars coming back to the United States through trade offset this country's outlays for Middle Eastern oil. . . .

US businessmen in the area are looking for investment opportunities as well as sales prospects. In Iran, E. I. Du Pont de Nemours is putting up its first grass-roots petrochemical complex outside the industrialized world, in a $280 million joint-venture fiber plant.

The role of private business is a barometer of the changes taking place. In Saudi Arabia, even the central planners are entrepreneurs at heart. Hisham Nazer, president of the Central Planning Organization [and former Saudi Arabian minister of state for planning], concedes that economic power is tilting toward the government . . . [in 1975] because official agencies are pouring oil revenues into roads, ports, housing. "But when it comes to building the real thing such as industry, we will try as much as we can to stay out," Nazer says, "or even after we are in, to get out."

Egypt's President Anwar Sadat, after taking office in 1970, started to reverse the trends toward militant nationalism and heavy Russian influence by throwing out the twenty thousand Soviet "advisers" brought in by former President [Gamal Abdel] Nasser. He has quietly abandoned Nasser's self-appointed role as the leader of Arab nationalism and of the third world. And he is cautiously reviving private business, suppressed by Nasser, while promoting US investment. [For additional information on Egyptian economic development, see "Egypt Rebuilds: Boom Time Along the Suez," in this section, below.]

Less noticed, but equally significant, are the changes in Syria's once doctrinaire Arab Socialist regime. President [Hafez] Assad is actively encouraging private business. He also renewed diplomatic relations with the United States . . . [in 1974], and an astonishing 500,000 Syrians trooped through a small American exhibit in a Damascus trade fair . . . [in August 1974]. . . .

Since then, the Syrians have started talks with GM [General Motors], Chrysler, and other auto makers about setting up an assembly plant. More surprising, Syria granted an offshore oil exploration concession in the Mediterranean . . . [in February 1974] to a US group headed by Tripco Petroleum, Inc.

Neighboring Iraq is not retreating from rigid socialism or loosening its political ties with the Soviet Union. But it is shifting its trade dramatically—away from the Soviet bloc and toward the West. After years of virtually no business contacts with the United States, the Iraqis are inviting Americans to Baghdad and signing big deals for everything from Boeing aircraft to Sheraton hotels. In another policy shift that eases a major source of political tension in the Middle East, Iraq has settled a thirty-seven-year border dispute with Iran.

The roots of these changes, in many cases, reach back before the oil bonanza. Nasser's bureaucracy-ridden Socialist regime, for example, ran down Egypt's economy and thereby "taught a lot of people what they do not want," observes a US businessman in Cairo. . . .

[In 1975] the oil riches pouring into the Middle East are reshaping political alignments as well as economic policies. Money from the [Persian] Gulf states is buying time for Sadat to try a new approach to Egypt's problems, and is smoothing Syria's transition to a more open economy.

The stepped-up flow of trade and investments among Arab countries is creating greater interdependence and putting new constraints on actions by individual nations. An example is the Riyadh-based Arab Investment Company, set up with $255 million of capital from ten governments to promote ventures with private investors. With so many governments as shareholders, says . . . the company's project manager, "our presence in any project is a guarantee against nationalization."

A Rotterdam-Teheran Traffic Jam

Enrico Borgonovi, a forty-three-year-old driver for Trasporti SATIM, a Milan trucking company, stood beside his looming Fiat 619 rig . . . , awaiting his turn to load. Ahead of him at the Milan loading dock of Hirsch-Iran, a freight forwarder, were a pair of five-axle Mercedes rigs with the name Hungaro-Camion blazoned on their flanks. The Hungarians were taking on mixed cargoes of medicinals and machinery. Behind Borgonovi were other big trucks lined up wheel-to-wheel.

Ahead of them all was a grueling, three-thousand-mile run from northern Italy to Teheran, Iran, along treacherous roads and snow-choked mountain passes in eastern Turkey.

"The last time I went through, the snow was piled three meters high," Borgonovi recalled. "In one night, I counted thirty trucks that had gone off the road."

Hairpin turns in mountain passes on rough roads, wide enough in places for only one truck to pass, are among the hazards in trucking to the Middle East from Europe through the Balkans and Turkey. There are others. Until . . . [late 1974] no trucker traveled alone through northern Iraq. On the run to Baghdad, trucks formed convoys and waited for Iraqi army escorts as protection against attacks by rebel Kurdish tribesmen.

Despite such problems, the trucking business between Western Europe and the Middle East is booming. Five hundred miles north of Milan, for example, Anthonius A. Schellekens, forty-seven, a driver for Dutch trucker G. M. De Roody & Sons, sets out every six weeks or so . . . at the wheel of a big vehicle carrier loaded with . . . cars and trucks for customers in Iran. Other drivers are hauling freight to the Middle East from factory loading docks all over Western Europe and from ports such as Rotterdam [the Netherlands], where cargoes from the United States are transshipped by truck.

The trucking bonanza is a spillover from the massive wave of imports, financed by oil dollars, that has created a hopeless shipping jam in Middle Eastern ports and has snarled rail traffic on overland routes. At almost every major harbor, from Beirut [Lebanon] on the Mediterranean to Jidda on the Red Sea and Basra [Iraq] at the head of the Persian Gulf, dozens of vessels are anchored offshore waiting to unload, and turnaround times have stretched to forty-five days—and more.

Chaos and Bottlenecks

For rail traffic moving to the Middle East through Turkey, only two ferries shuttle boxcars—fifteen at a time—across a mile-wide Bosporus [strait between Europe and Asia]. Another pair of ferries are the sole conveyances across Lake

Van, sixty miles wide and a mile above the sea level, in eastern Turkey. Even worse are the bottlenecks created by delays in customs clearance for rail freight moving from Turkey into Iraq, Iran, and Syria. To ease the pileup of freight cars on its eastern frontier, Turkey now limits transit traffic to four trains a day.

Meantime, Soviet railroads, which also have been hauling freight from Western Europe through the Caucasus to Iran, . . . halted all transit [in April 1975] for a week because hundreds of cars were piling up at Jolfa in the Armenian mountains on the Iranian border.

Such measures create havoc among shippers. Chrysler, for example, sent 160 knocked-down cars by sea from Britain to Hamburg [Germany] for transport to Iran by rail . . . Because of an earlier Soviet interruption of rail transit, the autos sat in German yards for four weeks and were finally rerouted by ship around Africa.

Eventually, the shipping tie-up in the Middle East should be eased by billions of dollars worth of new port construction and modernization. Several countries have plans for new railroads, too, although Saudi Arabia has not yet revived an often-discussed plan to rebuild a five-hundred-mile stretch of the railroad to Medina that was put out of commission . . . nearly sixty years ago [in World War I]. . . .

New Roles for the Oil Giants

Saudi Arabia's industrialization program "*has* to succeed," says John Hadjis, president of Texaco Saudia, Inc., in Riyadh. "And it is a must for us to be in it." It is also a must for Exxon, Mobil, and Standard Oil of California [Socal], Texaco's partners in Arabian American Oil Company (Aramco), and any other company that wants to assure itself of future supplies of Saudi crude oil.

The parent companies will lose their 40 percent share in the output of Aramco, the world's biggest crude oil producer, when negotiations are completed on a full takeover of Aramco by the Saudis, who . . . own 60 percent.

But the Saudis want help from the parent companies in setting up such projects as industrial plants, shipping ventures, and mining developments, and they are dangling long-term crude supplies as a carrot. "Those who give us more assistance will be allowed to lift more crude," says Sheik Ahmed Zaki Yamani, Saudi Arabia's minister of petroleum and mineral resources.

Rushing to comply, the Aramco partners have set up subsidiaries such as Texaco Saudia to launch joint ventures with the Saudi government. Proposed refineries will cost as much as $1 billion each.

The resulting relationship between the oil majors and the Saudis will be "a new pattern based on mutual interest, and it will create a financial interest for the companies in Saudi Arabia," Yamani says.

New patterns are also emerging in the oil business in other parts of the Middle East:

☐ Iran nationalized the fields formerly operated by a consortium of British, American, and French companies, but it continues to sell them most of the oil. Iran also pays a service company set up by the group to provide help in running the fields.

☐ The Iraqis, who are thought to have larger oil reserves than any country except Saudi Arabia, seized American shares in Basrah Petroleum, the country's biggest producer, during the 1973 [Arab-Israeli] war. They may eventually follow the Iranian pattern but seem in no hurry to take over the 57 percent still owned by the British and French.

☐ Abu Dhabi, which took over 60 percent of foreign oil operations, has backed off from plans to nationalize the remaining 40 percent, acknowledging that it needs the companies' help in running the industry.

☐ While other countries whittle down the oil companies' role, Egypt is bringing in twenty-four groups that plan to invest more than $500 million in a massive search for oil under production-sharing and "participation" agreements with the Egyptians.

Taking the Direct Approach

Thus, in one form or another, the international oil companies are going to be active throughout the Middle East for years to come. But for the Aramco partners, the key to their future is in Saudi Arabia. "We start, obviously, from the rationale that Saudi Arabia has some 30 percent of the world's probable oil reserves and is the biggest exporter," says W. Jack Butler, chairman of Mobil Saudi Arabia, Inc., with offices in the Queen's Center, Jidda's only high-rise office complex. "The oil industry is going through a restructuring, and as the government takes increasing control of Aramco it only makes good sense to develop a direct relationship in the country."

Yamani says the Aramco parents will have to pay the full market price for Saudi crude. Nevertheless, it is vital to them to have guaranteed, long-term supplies for their worldwide operations.

In the scramble to develop direct ties with Saudi Arabia, Mobil, the partner with the smallest share in Aramco, has a head start. It has marketed lubricants there since the turn of the century, and it operates an aircraft servicing business in partnership with Jidda's Alireza family. Currently, Mobil is setting up a Saudi shipping company with American and Saudi private partners headed by Prince Mohamed bin Fahd, the son of . . . Crown Prince [Fahd].

Mobil is also ahead of the other companies in setting up joint ventures with Petromin, the Saudi oil and industrial development agency. It has been a partner of Petromin in a lubricants blending plant for years and it is putting up a lube refinery with the agency. . . . Mobil [also] proposes to build a 250,000-barrel-per-day joint-venture refinery as well as a petrochemicals plant at Yenbo on the Red Sea.

In launching such projects, the Aramco partners are walking a tightrope because they are still negotiating the terms of the Aramco takeover by the government. One issue is the fees that the companies will be paid for continuing to supply technical and management help to Aramco.

The other big issue is the amount of Aramco's crude production that will be allotted to the parents. The companies could undercut their own bargaining position by appearing too eager to build costly plants in order to get additional crude supplies. . . .

Meantime, Texaco Saudia is negotiating a lube refinery and crude desulfurizing plant, jointly with Socal and Petromin, at Al Jubayl on the east coast. Exxon has studied projects ranging from shipping to copper and phosphate mining. Its biggest proposals are for a big ethane cracker and polyethylene complex and an export refinery.

Royal Dutch/Shell Group and Gulf Oil Corporation also are moving into Saudi Arabia with offers to build industrial plants. A petrochemical project of Shell Oil Company, the US affiliate of Royal Dutch/Shell, and a refinery proposal of Shell International are the first major ventures by any company to be formally approved by Petromin's board.

The partners in major petrochemical ventures, says Petromin Governor Abdulhady Hassan Taher, will be given a crude allotment of 250,000 to 350,000 barrels per day. But such quotas, tied to specific industrial ventures, are mere sweeteners. What Shell and other newcomers are really after, as a reward for helping the Saudis industrialize, is membership in the club of preferred customers for Saudi oil.

Profits Are a Must

Even so, the companies insist that the industrial ventures must be profitable. . . . This is a critical issue because building export plants in Saudi Arabia will cost 30 percent to 50 percent more than putting them in major markets such as Europe. The Saudis can offset these added costs with what amount to subsidies, and they seem prepared to pay the price in order to get the industry. . . .

One offset they are offering is cheap gas for fuel and feedstock. The key to industrialization, though, will probably be low-cost loans. The Shell projects are reported to be still hung up on financing arrangements. But the Saudis . . .

decided to offer fifteen-year loans to joint-venture partners at low interest for up to half the equity in the ventures. In some cases, that apparently means that foreign partners could borrow their entire shares of the capital. With such financing, the prospects for the new partnership between the oil companies and Saudi Arabia look bright.

OIL, GRANDEUR AND A CHALLENGE
TO THE WEST [2]

Ever since the oil crisis that rocked the world . . . [in 1973], the autocratic ruler of Iran has, to many people, indeed seemed to be basking in the light of the Almighty. Iran sits atop an estimated 60 billion barrels of crude oil, or roughly one tenth of the world's proven reserves. The disposition of "this noble product" (as Iranians like to call it), and the money to be made from it, is in the firm hands of one man: His Imperial Majesty Mohammed Reza Pahlevi, Aryamehr (Light of the Aryans), Shahanshah (King of Kings). Once dismissed by Western diplomats as an insecure, ineffective playboy-king, this emperor of oil commands new respect . . . , as much for his ambitions as for his wealth. By means of what he has called a "white revolution," the shah is determined to transform Iran, a country that still includes nomads whose life-style has not changed in a thousand years, into a Middle Eastern superpower.

Iran . . . [in 1974] has a unique position in the world: it is a Moslem nation but not an Arab one. Yet it plays a key role in the power politics of the Middle East, without being directly involved in the struggles between Israel and its Arab neighbors. Iran has a proud past and almost unlimited future potential, which the shah intends to develop with his new-found oil wealth. . . . He has consistently argued for keeping prices high—essential, he believes, if the countries of the Middle East are ever to achieve the high standard of

[2] From article in *Time*. 104:28-33+. N. 4, '74. Reprinted by permission from *Time*, the Weekly Newsmagazine; Copyright Time Inc.

living taken for granted in the West. Laudable though that ambition may be, many Western leaders find it hard to accept the shah's argument, especially since he frequently combines it with moralizing messages about the need for industrial nations to scrimp and economize. Iran is one of the handful of nations that has helped push Western Europe to the edge of economic disaster—and has begun a major redistribution of wealth. Whether he is seen as hero or villain, the shah cannot be ignored. . . .

In the eyes of Iran's 32 million people, the prosperity and national prestige the shah is bringing them has bathed their ruler with new luster. Thus . . . [when the shah] celebrated his fifty-fifth birthday [in 1974]—his fifty-sixth by Iranian reckoning, which counts the day of birth as one's first birthday—the national holiday was observed with particular fervor. The capital city of Teheran (population 3.8 million) glowed from the light of millions of colored lamps. As part of the festivities, the shah and . . . Empress Farah reviewed a mass exhibition of gymnasts in the $185 million sports complex built for the . . . Asian Games. The shah also grandly pardoned 148 prisoners who had been convicted of such charges as robbery, drug use, antistate activities and "plots against the monarchy."

Another and perhaps more impressive affirmation of the shah's position in Iranian life took place at Golestan Palace. He presided over a *salam* or birthday levee of a thousand courtiers and high officials. . . . At a signal from the master of ceremonies, they carried out a prescribed ritual: a bow, a kiss bestowed on the outstretched imperial hand and flowery salutations, *"Tavalod-e-Shahanshah Aryamehr ra Tabrik Arz Mikonam* [Greetings on your Imperial Majesty's birthday]."

In the . . . [thirty-fourth] year of an often uncertain reign, Mohammed Reza Pahlevi has brought Iran to a threshold of grandeur that is at least analogous to what Cyrus the Great achieved for ancient Persia. Items:

☐ Iran is . . . producing 6.1 million barrels of oil daily and is the world's second-greatest oil-exporting nation, after Saudi Arabia. Iran's refinery at Abadan is the world's largest. More important, the shah was one of the first oil potentates to take complete control of production and reserves: since 1954 all income from production has gone to the National Iranian Oil Company, which is completely controlled by his government.

☐ Iran's oil revenues are increasing astronomically. Technocrats working on the country's latest five-year development plan have been forced to rejiggle the revenue side of the ledger almost daily; it now stands at $23 billion in oil income . . . [in 1974], versus $5 billion . . . [in 1973]. . . .

☐ Unlike Saudi Arabia, whose resources are almost inexhaustible, Iran is expending both its oil and its oil income to create a broad industrial base in the country before the crude begins to run out (1990, by Iranian estimates). That involves a heavy investment in social development, since 40 percent of Iranians are illiterate. Outside the cities, many live in poverty; about 85 percent of Iran's land is untillable without artificial irrigation. . . . [In 1974 Iran spent] $16 billion on projects ranging from dams to schools to hospitals. By the end of the current five-year plan, the shah will have spent more than $68 billion on domestic improvements.

☐ With excess oil income, Iran is also undertaking aid and investment abroad. . . . [1974's] expenditures include $700 million to the International Monetary Fund to assist nations with balance of payment problems and $350 million to the World Bank. Additionally, [in 1974] Iran . . . has committed $7 billion worth of grants, loan and deposits against future purchases from a dozen countries, including Britain and France. For an estimated $100 million, the government . . . bought 25.04 percent ownership of the steel-producing branch of West Germany's 162-year-old Krupp steel empire. In August [1974] the shah endowed a million-dollar chair in petroleum engineering at the University of Southern California.

No other member of the club of suddenly wealthy oil

nations is advanced enough or populous enough to match
Iran's [1990] projected scale of social and economic growth.
... Certainly no other oil power has a leader quite as visionary and energetic in his planning. Even though the shah's
ambitious plans for Iran are barely under way, the country
has already achieved such a preeminent place in the Middle
East that businessmen and diplomats alike are beating a jet-
pattern path to the shah's door.

Great Civilization

Important visitors, naturally, are granted audiences with
the man who makes the decisions. The shah was educated in
Switzerland and has traveled widely abroad; he converses
with his visitors as fluently in French or English as in Farsi,
the principal Iranian language. In any of the three tongues,
he can evangelistically describe his goals for Iran's Great
Civilization—a phrase redolent of the American New Frontier and Great Society of the 1960s. When the civilization
matures, the shah believes, it will turn Iran into the "Japan
of West Asia" ...

Already oil money has begun to transform Iran into an
empire of paradoxes. The old Persia remains for those who
seek it: the Qashqai tribe in the southwest still graze their
cattle in the Zagros Mountains and locate water in a 1,000-
year-old system of interconnected wells known as *qanats*.
In Teheran entrepreneurs who make $50,000 a day take jet
flights to Europe to complete a business deal (and see
banned-in-Iran movies like *Last Tango in Paris*) or perhaps
buy a vacation villa. ...

Some of the wives of these new middle-class millionaires,
who celebrate Women's Emancipation Day each February
and can divorce their husbands as easily as men once could
divorce wives under Islamic law, are dressed by [fashion de-
signers Cristóbal] Balenciaga and [Christian] Dior. But on
the street they pass other women who still wear the traditional speckled *chador,* or robe of modesty. The bustling
streets of Teheran are so clogged with automobiles, includ-

ing the made-in-Iran Paykan (Hillman) and Chevrolet Iran (Opel) as well as double-decked Leyland transit buses, that the city has belatedly begun to consider building a mass-transit system.

Contradiction leaps out everywhere in Iran. . . . In Teheran, the mud huts of the poor lie hard by the condominiums of the rich. In the bazaars of Isfahan, a merchant accustomed to dealing with Iranians is likely to find himself negotiating simultaneously with a Russian steel mill technician and an American helicopter expert.

The glue that holds this disparate society together is the Shahanshah. "Who built your new mosque?" the headman of the village of Hesar Khorvan on the slopes of the Elburz Mountains is asked. "The shah, of course," he answers firmly. For the bourgeois Teherani, the shah has grown to be a kind of imperial security blanket. . . .

The shah's underlying aim in building his Great Civilization is to make Iran not only secure but self-sufficient. "Since World War II," says Premier Amir-Abbas Hoveida, "we have seen that pacts and bilateral arrangements don't work when you need them. Our buildup is our only way of survival." The shah is succeeding so adroitly that even old adversaries look at him with respect. The Arab states of the Persian Gulf, who share nothing culturally with Iran but religion, are apprehensive about the massive military power the shah has been building up with oil income. At the same time, they are pleased with the shah's insistence on higher oil prices.

The Soviet Union, which during World War II occupied and attempted to annex Iran's northernmost province of Azerbaijan, is . . . [in 1974] almost purringly cooperative. Moscow has toned down the anti-shah propaganda it formerly beamed forth as a way of promoting Iran's outlawed Communist (Tudeh) party. In exchange for Iranian natural gas, which is piped over the border from Aga-jari, the Soviets constructed Iran's first super steel plant at Isfahan . . . only twenty-four miles from an American-staffed helicopter school that is the world's largest. Relations with Moscow are so correct . . . that the Russians made no complaints when the shah . . . [in 1974] raised the price of natural gas from 30.7 cents per 1,000 cubic foot to 57 cents.

The shah considers himself a good friend of the United States. Indeed, relations between Washington and Teheran have generally been excellent since 1953, when the CIA [Central Intelligence Agency] fomented demonstrations that led to a coup against the late leftist Premier Mohammed Mossadegh, thereby allowing the fledgling shah to return to power after a brief, humiliating exile in Rome. . . . However, there is more than a single view of the shah in official Washington, and sometimes he is given to wondering which one reflects the real government position.

Hired Gun

At the Treasury Department, for instance, the shah is generally thought of as a tyrant and a megalomaniac whose stubbornness and greed over oil prices represent a threat to the economic stability of the world. . . . The shah is somewhat more highly regarded at the Pentagon. The Defense Department is pleased with the shah's massive purchases of sophisticated US weapons, but some intelligence analysts cynically regard the shah as little more than America's hired gun in the Middle East. At the State Department, by contrast, the shah is considered an enlightened ruler who is propelling his backward people into prosperity and is defending his own country, as well as US interests, against the spread of communism.

What makes the shah a key figure in the Middle East, some US diplomats believe, is the fact that like Secretary of State [Henry] Kissinger, he has managed to deal equably with both sides. He considers the Israelis arrogant and even "masochistic." But Iran nevertheless provides Israel with 50 percent of its oil. In return, Israeli experts on irrigation and land reclamation have transformed İran's Ghazvin Plain into a fertile oasis. At the same time, the shah responded favorably . . . [in October 1973] to a request from Saudi Arabia's [late] King Faisal and dispatched six Iranian air force C-130 transports to ferry Saudi troops and equipment to the war against Israel. . . .

Hard Words

The shah, whose government will spend $1 billion . . . [in 1974] to subsidize imports of meat, wheat, sugar and soybeans, insists that rising oil prices are no different than rising commodity prices. He seeks to tie the two together in an economic index that would help to limit further increases. The US position is that oil is artificially priced, which the shah himself admits, while agricultural increases are a response to free market conditions. President Ford, and Kissinger in . . . [a] United Nations speech, abruptly cautioned the oil-producing nations not to price their product at disastrously high levels. The shah, more accustomed to hand kissing than hard words, bristled. "Nobody can dictate to us," he told newsmen on a state visit to Australia and New Zealand. "Nobody can wave a finger at us because we will wave back." . . . The shah warned, "If this is a serious policy of the US government, then on this subject we are going to have a very serious clash."

When the shah talks about clashes these days, other nations sit up and take notice. Undeniably, Iran is becoming one of the world's major military powers. To equip his 160,000-man army, 40,000-man air force and 11,500-man navy, the shah . . . contracted for such imposingly modern weapons as 70 US F-4 Phantom jets, 800 British Chieftain tanks and an assortment of destroyers, hovercraft and troop-transport planes. In a deal that probably saved Long Island's Grumman Aircraft Corporation from bankruptcy, the shah . . . [in 1974] ordered 80 F-14s at a cost of nearly $1.5 billion. By 1980 Iran will have more fighter-bombers (839) than any NATO [North Atlantic Treaty Organization] nation except the United States. The shah, a skilled pilot with more than

5,000 flying hours in fixed-wing aircraft and helicopters to his credit, insisted on checking out the Phantoms personally.

Jugular Vein

Some of Iran's Arab neighbors wonder whether the shah really needs all that expensive hardware and worry about his ambitions. . . . In answer, Iranians point out that they share a 1,100-mile border with the Soviet Union; and the Russians, they argue, have never really given up their interest in gaining control of Iran's oil fields some day. Iran also has an inimical and testy neighbor in Iraq, which has been massively supplied with Soviet weaponry. The forces of the two states frequently clash head-on along the border. In the most recent skirmish . . . [in spring 1974], Iran lost 42 men in a fierce firefight but killed at least 39 Iraqis in return.

The shah maintains that he is building a force with the primary mission of protecting Arabs and Iranians alike in the Persian Gulf, from which 86 percent of the non-Communist world's crude shipments originate. The gulf at its neck narrows until the supertanker channel is only twelve miles wide at the Strait of Hormuz, which Premier Hoveida calls "our jugular vein." Iran worries that dissident forces, like the radical Popular Front for the Liberation of Oman, which is currently fighting Sultan Qabus [ibn Said] in Oman, could block the strait by sinking a supertanker. The shah's response has been a pride of military powers so vast that he not only can neutralize the guerrillas but also dominate the gulf. Says one US diplomat: "The Arabs like to call it the Arabian Gulf. But it really is the Persian Gulf. It's the shah's lake."

A well-equipped military loyal to the shah would also be helpful in putting down any dissident uprising within Iran. The emperor freely admits that opposition to the monarchy is not tolerated in Iran, and he has methodically repressed dissent. His principal instrument for maintaining internal security, as he sees it, is SAVAK, Iran's feared secret police organization which routinely scrutinizes even job applications and requests for exit visas. . . . The shah himself insists that SAVAK is not large, and some Western observers in Teheran wonder whether it is as efficient as Iranians believe. Nevertheless, the secret police, through a large network of informers, have been responsible for making countless arrests of leftists on occasionally vague and anti-shah charges and for at least two hundred executions. The shah, who has twice been a target of assassination attempts, travels with a heavy security guard and makes fewer public appearances . . .

If the shah has both strong intimations of mortality and a divine sense of mission, it may well be because his dynasty is of surprisingly recent origin. His father, Reza Shah, was a swaggering forty-five-year-old army major in 1921 when he seized power from the corrupt Qajar dynasty. Harsh and intractable, Reza Shah was unable to cope with the world powers that interfered in Persian affairs after oil was discovered. Finally, in 1941, on the ground that he had become dangerously friendly with the Hitler regime, Reza Shah was packed off to exile in South Africa by the British and Russians. The throne passed to his shy, diffident twenty-two-year-old son.

In his first years on the throne, the shah was generally considered a figurehead monarch who cared more for fast cars, fancy living and pretty women than for the tasks of kingship. That impression was reinforced by his failure to deal firmly with Premier Mossadegh during the 1950s, and by his ineffectual early struggles with the landowning "thousand families" who largely controlled his country. In 1950 he attempted unsuccessfully to force them to hand over their land to their peasants; the shah set an example by deeding 450,000 acres of crown property to the 42,000 farmers who worked the royal farms.

Not until 1963, when he undertook Iran's white revolution (now officially known as the Revolution of the Shah and the People), was he able to break the power of the landlords and smash the vestiges of feudalism that paralyzed the country. The move gave him fresh strength from a new base of support in the middle and lower classes. Confident of his power, the shah in 1967 finally decreed his coronation—after twenty-six years on the throne. . . .

Theoretically at least, Iran is a constitutional monarchy, with a parliament consisting of the Majlis or lower house and a Senate and premier. In fact, the shah is one of the world's few remaining absolute monarchs. He guides all of Iran's essential business and makes the final decisions Searching for a comparison to the shah's power, Premier Hoveida considers the most recent parallel to have been the French presidency under Charles de Gaulle. "Parliament does not impede the executive," Hoveida explains, "so we have a more efficient system and there is a dialogue."

To stress the strength of the throne, Iran lays heavy emphasis on kingly privilege. Not only do aides, including the premier, kiss his hand, but peasants also kiss his feet as a mark of respect. When the shah stands, everyone in his presence also stands until he sits again. Iranian public works, from the 609-foot-tall Mohammed Reza Pahlevi dam. Iran's highest, to the Aryamehr steel complex, are named in honor of the shah or the shahbanou. "The outside world thinks that we want that sort of thing," said Empress Farah . . . "We don't. But people want it, and if we don't accede they think we are not interested." In the most lavish display of opulence in Iranian memory, the shah . . . [in 1971] celebrated 2,500 years of Persian empire with a $100 million extravaganza at Persepolis [site of the vast ruins of the ancient capital of Persia], attended by Ethiopia's Emperor Haile Selassie, nine other kings and sixteen presidents. . . .

Inside Iran, where the alert ears of SAVAK may be tuned toward caustic remarks, there is little open criticism of the way in which the shah is building his Great Civilization Outside Iran his development has been praised by the United Nations. . . . But there is also skepticism not so much about the laudable end of the shah's programs but about the means.

Allergic to Caviar

The most pointed criticism is that a nation of 32 million people cannot possibly be drawn into the technocratic twenty-first century by the fiat of a single man, no matter how good his intentions. The shah . . . is in good health—his worst indisposition, ironically, is an allergy that prevents his eating Iran's world-famous Caspian caviar—and he works a fifteen-hour day with scant time out for family life. But for all the shah's skill and experience, sooner or later decisions must be shared more than they have been up to now.

One reason why so much power is kept in imperial hands is that Iran has a dangerously small pool of trusted technocrats capable of running the country. The armed forces, which have a lavish pay scale matching those of most corporations, constantly vie with private industry for talent. Universities have room for only one of every ten hopeful students who apply. The shah's immediate circle of advisers is also surprisingly small. Among them are Premier Hoveida, . . . a dapper man who has held his job . . . [ten] years; Hushang Ansary, . . . minister of economic affairs and finance; Amir Assadullah Alam, . . . who acts as the sovereign's right hand as minister of the court; and Jamshid Amuzegar, . . . who until recently served as the shah's voice and goad at OPEC [Organization of Petroleum Exporting Countries] meetings. . . .

Far from having limitless funds to finance both a growing army and an expanding economy, the country will actually soon be capital-short. . . . Already some inadequacies in rapid economic growth are becoming clear. The five-year plan by 1978 will create 2.1 million additional jobs. But there will be only 1.4 million Iranians qualified to fill them. That opens up the prospect of importing vast numbers of guest workers from other nations, as Western European powers do. Iranians are not sure they like the idea. There are sizable groups of foreigners in Iran already; the US community, many members of which work on military-assistance programs (and who refer to the shah as "Ralph" in conversations that his secret police might find critical, and thus unconstitutional), is already 15,000 strong. . . .

[In October 1974] the shah decreed free and compulsory elementary school education throughout the country. The problem, however, is that Iran does not have enough teachers. One reasonably successful palliative up to now has been the creation of a "literacy corps" of high school graduates who spend most of their two-year military service teaching school. The corps has a program in which teachers travel with nomadic tribesmen and at each stop pitch a white school tent alongside the tribes' black goat-hair tents. The shah also decided that each schoolchild should have a free daily glass of milk—an impossible task for the country's modest dairy industry. Even imported powdered milk would not improve the situation.

Iran's expanding economy, moreover, might easily be strangled by a tradition of bureaucratic bungling and red tape. Simply to retrieve an incoming air-freight package from Teheran's international airport requires thirteen signatures from as many offices, a process that takes about three hours. A Teheran resident, complying with the law by paying an additional $1.20 tax assessment not long ago, had to try for nearly a month before he found the appropriate offices and could fill out the proper forms. "A thousand-rial [$13] bribe would have settled it in three minutes," he said bitterly.

One byproduct of such bureaucracy, as the shah is aware, is corruption. Foreigners flocking to Iran to do business have discovered that even in the army, payoffs have been demanded. Only at the very top, apparently, is there total honesty. But crackdowns have begun. . . .

Another aspect of Iran's development that bothers critics is the shah's unstated decision that political progress for the time being must take second place to economic growth. Decentralization of political power is moving slowly, and there is scant evidence of any quick shift from benevolent but absolute monarchy to at least limited democracy. Theoretically, Iran is a nation of competing political parties. Hoveida's Iran Novin (New Iran) holds power with a dominating 235 seats in the 267-seat Majlis. But Mardom (The People's party), which has all but one of the remaining seats, was created on the shah's order as a kind of loyal opposition. As it is, neither party is outspoken or forceful. . . . Younger Iranians chafe at such restrictions, but the government is in no hurry to change the situation. . . .

Convinced that change is impossible, many students simply remain abroad after they complete foreign studies, even though the shah's social-minded program is as ambitious as anything they could prescribe for Iran. The shortage in doctors—presently 22,000—could be nearly wiped out merely if all the Iranian doctors living in the United States would come home again.

In contrast with the dissident young, older Iranians appear to have accepted the priorities. In place of political freedom, they are willing to accept a stunning improvement in their life-styles. . . . As the middle class is uneasily aware, Iran's new prosperity is unevenly shared. A scant 10 percent of the people control 40 percent of the wealth, while the bottom 30 percent enjoy only 8 percent of it. Inflation, now running at 20 percent, diminishes even these gains. Until the situation improves, the shah's white revolution will be incomplete.

In moments of reflection, the shah has been known to confess some unease about aspects of his Great Civilization. He worries in particular about the contamination of Iran's proud cultural heritage by modern life. In fact, there is an untrammeled kind of frontier spirit on the loose in Iran today; past heritage is being bulldozed into rubble as the country tries to build a future.

Grand Goals

But there are larger questions about Iran's future that remain unanswered. What if the shah were to die suddenly?

Would Empress Farah, who has been designated regent for Crown Prince Reza, fourteen, be able to carry on the great projects now under way? Is the shah's imposing military buildup a deterrent against war or a provocation? The shah has not only filled the power vacuum that existed in the gulf after the British left but has shown an interest in establishing a strong naval presence in the Indian Ocean. Inevitably, such a move would increase the fears of Iran's neighbors about the shah's geopolitical ambitions. Will the people and, above all, the army remain loyal if the grand goals of the white revolution are unrealized and if untrammeled economic progress outstrips social growth? After all, some are still alive who witnessed the ouster of the last monarch but one by an ambitious, dissatisfied soldier. On the record so far, the future favors the shah. Between oil and ambition, therefore, he and his developing nation are bound to be increasingly visible, increasingly vocal and increasingly vital.

EGYPT REBUILDS: BOOM TIME ALONG THE SUEZ [3]

A few stumpy palm trees struggling to grow out of the dusty rubble, and here and there a Mediterranean red tile roof standing atop the burned-out shell of a house—these are all that remain of the once pleasant community of Port Taufiq. Before the 1967 war with Israel, 80,000 Egyptians lived in this suburb of Suez City, where the Suez Canal Authority had its headquarters. . . . [In 1975] it is ruined and completely abandoned, a symbol of the gigantic reconstruction task Egypt is facing along its war-battered canal zone.

But . . . [more than] two years have passed since the fateful [1973] canal crossing which silenced the Israeli cannons that had been pounding away from the Sinai, and now, on the other edge of Suez City, another kind of symbol is

[3] From article by Larry Diamond, a member of a graduate program in sociology at Stanford University; freelance writer. *Nation*. 220:680-4. Je. 7, '75. Reprinted by permission.

rising rapidly in the desert. In three eight-hour shifts each day, workmen are rushing to complete a sprawling complex of attractive pink stucco and stone apartment buildings. Nine different companies, 11,000 men and $30 million of Saudi Arabian oil revenues are working to construct King Faisal City, a model residential community that will ultimately house 24,000 people. It is to be only the first of many such projects in Egypt, part of a development scheme designed to remake the Suez Canal Zone into a major center of world commerce, transform its beaches into one of the world's top resort attractions, and catapult its economy into the front ranks of third world industrial powers.

Behind the grandiose rebuilding schemes is a short, squat, intense businessman with a gift for visionary planning and a military-command flair for getting things done in a hurry. When Osman Ahmed Osman, the largest private contractor in the Arab world, moved in as Egypt's minister of reconstruction . . . [in late 1973], he brought with him sweeping authority from President Sadat to by-pass the swollen bureaucracy and run his ministry as he did his business. Now the results of this unorthodox arrangement are beginning to emerge. . . .

[Since 1974] roads, houses, water supply, sewage and power systems have been sufficiently restored in the cities of the canal zone to enable the [1967] war refugees to return to the region. In some cases, the massive construction projects under way have attracted populations larger than those of the pre-1967 war. Port Said, at the northern end of the canal, now has 310,000 people, 50,000 more than its prewar level. Ismailia's population stands today at 180,000—40,000 more than it once had.

The long-range development plan for the canal zone is staggeringly ambitious; it will require $10 billion . . . [by 1980] to recreate Port Said, Ismailia and Suez City as jet-age commercial, industrial and tourist centers, linked by six-lane highways and modern rail lines running through a one-hundred-mile strip of new industries and agricultural plots that will extend all the way down both sides of the canal. The immediate goals are to revitalize the economy and relieve the crippling human pressure on Cairo, and Osman thinks it possible to complete half of the major long-range projects within five years. . . . [In 1975] alone $1.5 billion is scheduled for investment in the infrastructure and housing needed to support the new economic life of the area. By the year's end, the dozen consulting firms now drawing up specific master plans for each city will have completed their work, and construction of the new manufacturing plants will begin.

Most of those plants will be in the ultramodern new free zone areas to be established in Suez and Port Said at either end of the canal. They are intended to lure industry and trade with freedom from taxes and customs, special investment credits, cheap labor, strategic location and only a token tariff for use of the harbors. Massive expansion of each harbor will . . . begin, at a cost of $400 million, to prepare them for the vastly increased traffic.

Minister Osman plans to concentrate in Suez and Port Said the types of industry for which raw materials lie in abundance within easy reach. Thus Suez City will be a major center for oil refining, mineral and fish processing and the production of cement, fertilizer and petrochemicals. Port Said, which will have its urban area increased sevenfold, will feature shipbuilding, textiles and fishing-related industries, as well as manufacturing and assembly plants.

In addition, Osman envisions Port Said, with access to both canal and the Mediterranean, becoming one of the major trading centers of the world. Already several African countries have submitted proposals to build storage depots there for their cocoa, timber and other exports. "Where else on earth," asks one economic planner with a gleam in his eye, "could you find a better site to link the markets of Europe, Africa and the Far East?"

Ismailia is to be developed into a major tourist and resort center, growing around the unspoiled beaches of Lake

Timsah in the canal. It will also become the agro-industrial center of Egypt. Half a million acres of desert land will be reclaimed around it and dedicated to a style of agriculture new to Egypt—fruits, vegetables and seed oils that will be canned for export.

The expansion of the canal itself . . . is already proceeding in a three-year, first-stage program that will cost almost $700 million and will more than double the canal's width, to accept 150,000-ton tankers fully loaded. A Japanese construction firm will . . . begin excavating what will amount to four times the volume of earth moved to create the original canal. And American and European engineering consultants are about to submit their studies on the economic and technical feasibility of a second three-year, $700 million widening of the canal which would excavate ten times the original volume of earth and accommodate 250,000-ton supertankers full of oil. However, until new tolls for the canal are set, there is no assurance that the shippers will find the reopened shortcut more attractive than the route around the tip of Africa that they have been using . . . [since the canal closed in 1967]. In any case, for some time to come the giant tankers will be rounding the Cape of Good Hope.

Three tunnels, one near each city, will pass beneath the canal for automobile and truck traffic. Construction on the first, at Suez City . . . could be completed . . . [by 1978]. A quarter of a million acres will be irrigated on the east bank, and it is believed that ultimately as many as 800,000 acres could be reclaimed in the Sinai desert. In fact, when and if the bulk of the Sinai is regained [from Israel], officials in the Reconstruction Ministry are ready to extend the central Ismailia irrigation canal across the Suez and deep into the peninsula.

And the plans by no means stop there. "If we regain the Sinai," said one high official in the ministry recently, "we are going to settle it sufficiently to insure that it is never taken again." Osman has in mind a grand design for the Sinai that involves spending $5 billion . . . [by 1985] to enlarge the present population of 100,000 on the peninsula to two million, establishing not only new farms but new industries, mines and processing plants.

Osman and his team of engineers and architects are also looking west of the canal into the desert between Cairo and Ismailia. Midway between these two cities they are preparing to build from scratch an industrial city of some 250,000 residents (ultimately half a million) that would further relieve the pressure of people streaming into Cairo looking for work. A Swedish firm has the planning well under way and construction . . . [began] in the middle of the year [1975]. Planners believe the new city will attract foreign firms because of its particularly abundant supply of cheap labor and its proximity to both Cairo and Port Said. Goodyear and Michelin are among the foreign companies said to be interested.

Foreign investment will be the pivotal element not only in the development of the industrial city and canal zone but in the revitalization and future growth of the entire economy. "The days of [the late Egyptian President Gamal Abdel] Nasser's swashbuckling, tough-talking socialism are at an end," said one foreign businessman. "[President Anwar] Sadat is determined to provide a secure climate for investments." Withdrawal from the spirit of Nasser's nationalization campaigns is . . . regarded as irreversible for far into the political future. Last June [1974] a new foreign investments law was approved that not only guarantees investments against seizure or nationalization but sweetens the pot in some rather extraordinary ways. New foreign investments will enjoy a tax holiday for their first five years of operation in Egypt—and this boon can be extended for up to eight years. Firms may also be granted exemption from customs duties for industrial machinery that they import. And investors will be allowed immediately to transfer home their entire share of profits, and to repatriate their capital after five years of work, if they so wish.

Such liberal terms are attracting the interest of a sweeping array of major foreign concerns. Egypt is eager to involve them in a host of specific joint-venture projects, and is looking with especially high hopes to the capital and technology of American firms. The Ministry of Industry has been talking with General Motors about a $65 million auto assembly plant and a $100 million plant for heavy trucks and buses; with American Motors about a plant for vans and microbuses; with United States Steel about a phosphate acid plant. The Ministry of Petroleum has been negotiating with Union Carbide for a giant petrochemical complex in Alexandria; with W. R. Grace for an aromatics complex; and with Gulf Oil for a plant to produce lubricating oil.

Already, foreign capital is flowing into twenty joint ventures which were approved . . . [in 1974]. Japan and Brazil will participate in constructing a $100 million sponge iron factory; Qatar will be Egypt's partner in a $65 million polyester fibers plant; Iraq and England will participate in producing farm tractors. And Kuwait will be half owner in a string of schemes ranging from production of cement, sheet glass and paper pulp to urban housing, tourist hotels and maritime transportation. In fact, Kuwait's total investment in Egypt [by 1980] through loans and joint ventures will total $1.4 billion . . . —almost half of the total $3 billion in investment commitments from the Arab world for that period. Added to this will be another $1 billion . . . pledged by the shah of Iran for joint-venture projects.

Egypt is equally desirous of the technical and financial involvement of Western Europe. Sadat . . . made a grand state visit to Paris, wooing France to participate in a wide range of development projects. In addition to the prominently displayed military agreement, the two nations announced a major economic cooperation package in which France will aid in building a $90 million power station at Abukir, near Alexandria, a petrochemical complex, a beet sugar factory, production plants for cement and fertilizer and a number of tourist schemes. French technology will be used to introduce a color television system in Egypt, and will combine with Arab capital to produce insecticides, vehicles, steel and building materials.

There are plans on even grander scales. Egypt hopes . . . to sign contracts with France, the United States and the Soviet Union for nuclear power stations that could be operational . . . [by the mid-1980s]. And the government is now studying with West Germany the potential power generating capacity of the huge Qattara Depression in the western desert. The project, agreed upon in principle, is likely to cost $1 billion and take ten years to complete. It would bring sea water from the Mediterranean down into the desert depression through a forty-mile canal. Officials feel it could eventually produce ten times the electric energy generated by the Aswan High Dam.

The appeals for foreign capital are mandated by a need that is overwhelming by any standard. Ambassador Tahseen Basheer, President Sadat's chief press adviser, estimates that to raise the present per capita income of $120 to just $200 would require $40 billion of foreign investment . . . [by 1980]. The needs of the country demand now a flexible kind of socialism, he argues. "Our socialism must not be a program to make people suffer because of a self-righteous attitude."

Private Egyptian capital is also beginning to be rehabilitated and encouraged in the new liberal climate. A base of private enterprise still remains, concentrated in the textile and construction industries, and in small factories. And . . . a number of Egyptian entrepreneurs, forced to flee at the height of Nasser's nationalization campaign, are sounding out the feasibility of returning to Egypt. . . .

There is no more illustrious symbol of the returning entrepreneurial spirit than Minister Osman Ahmed Osman himself, who has built his construction company into a giant multimillion-dollar conglomerate with branches in nine Arab nations and a total labor force of more than 23,000. Contemptuous of socialism for failing to develop anything more than "words and speeches and bureaucracy," Osman is eager to attract foreign capital from every part of the globe. "I want foreign investment to profit here. If they profit, Egypt profits."

The swing back toward a more mixed economy could pick up steam . . . with the limited reopening of the long-defunct Cairo stock exchange. The finance minister is . . . considering this step, with strict controls to protect the many small investors who would be buying stock for the first time. In a possible precursor of such a move, Egypt will make available to private owners 15 percent of its one-half share in a new $20 million joint investment fund with Saudi Arabia. To soothe the inevitable objections of entrenched public-sector bureaucrats to this "invasion" of foreign and private capital, many of the managers of state companies will be given chairmanships of the new joint-venture firms, with appropriate increases in salary and benefits.

"Invasion" it might well be called. For many months . . . [in early 1975] Cairo has been a city buzzing daily with news of the comings and goings of foreign government and business delegations. In the space of one week here . . . the minister of economic cooperation received delegations from Britain, Italy, Germany, Switzerland, Norway, the United States, Japan and Australia, bringing with them suggestions for joint projects in industry, commerce and tourism.

This stream of high-level businessmen and technicians whirling through the downtown hotels and government ministries has whipped up inevitable expectations of an economic boom. But for the short run, at least, it is unlikely. In fact, one exasperated American observer finds such expectations totally unrealistic in as poor a country as Egypt, "where there isn't even the money to fill the potholes in the streets, and the walls of government buildings are just peeling away." . . .

Even more than the dual shortage of basic food items and the liquid cash to pay for them, the shoddy state of the economy's infrastructure may well be the most crippling short-term obstacle to development. Streets, highways, rail-roads, buses, ports, telecommunications, electricity—every kind of service on which industrial expansion must depend is in an advanced state of disrepair and at least twenty years out of date. And it is by no means clear that the money will be available to upgrade these decaying systems. Foreign in-vestors are unlikely to find in such basic development proj-ects the high rate of return they seek. . . .

Minister Osman claims that the Arab neighbors have so far come through with important contributions toward de-veloping basic services in the canal zone, and adds with supreme confidence, "Give me a good design from top plan-ners and I will have no problem financing it." True perhaps for his glamorous canal zone projects, but little relief for the hard-pressed service sectors of Cairo and Alexandria.

There are some hopeful signs in the long-term economic picture, which promise a dramatic increase in Egypt's for-eign currency earnings. One is the Suez Canal, which is ex-pected to bring in $350 million a year—again assuming that it can compete with the longer voyage around Africa. There is the huge sponge iron industry . . . being developed, the exports from which planners believe could earn $300 million annually when full production is achieved in the 1980s. In the southwestern desert lie more than a billion tons in proven reserves of phosphates, with which Egypt hopes to become a net exporter of several million tons of fertilizer a year. By 1981, that would begin to earn at least another $300 million a year.

And Egypt is now scouring its shores and deserts for the most profitable of all natural resources—oil. Twenty-seven exploration contracts have been signed at a cost of almost $1 billion. By . . . [the 1980s] Egypt hopes to have discov-ered enough oil to be producing at a rate of more than a million barrels a day.

Plans are also being readied to turn the country's long, untouched northern coastline west of Alexandria into one of the resort capitals of the world. A British firm was

. . . granted a $220 million contract to develop Ras el Heikmah, 130 miles west of Alexandria, into a sprawling resort complex with golf courses, inland recreation, water sports, night clubs, ultramodern hotels and private villas. With its crystal-blue water, fine white sand and rich backdrop of natural vegetation, it will become, says one of its planners, "just like a piece of the Riviera." And capital is pouring into Egypt to modernize its tourism industry all over the country. . . . [In late 1974] an Egyptian-Saudi Arabian joint stock company was formed just to build hotels. Other Arab countries and international firms like Pan American are readying plans to cash in on what is seen as a tourism bonanza. The Ministry of Tourism feels that by 1980 the number of tourists can be increased from 700,000 to 2 million. Such an increase would at least triple Egypt's tourism income to $500 million a year.

If these projections sound like the makings of a long-term economic transformation, there persist grave doubts that it will ever be realized. For on the path toward the double-digit economic growth envisioned by the planners . . . lie mammoth problems that threaten to swallow up the huge amounts of human and financial capital that will be needed. For one, Egypt is suffering from a severe emigration that is carrying away thousands of its best scientists, doctors, teachers, engineers and skilled workers every year. Lured to Europe, North America and neighboring Arab states by substantially higher salaries, they are often never seen again. With an excellent university system now training 300,000 students, few doubt that Egypt can produce the administrative and technical talent it needs—if only it can hold on to them once they are trained.

The solution is as obvious as the problem is severe: higher pay. And some progress is being made in the canal zone, where Osman has raised construction wages enormously and is beginning to draw back from other Arab countries the engineers and carpenters and other skilled construction workers he needs. In the state industries pressure is mounting to raise salary scales all along the line, but it is felt that this must be linked to a comparable rise in output, which runs the problem into a kind of vicious circle. Government planning officials are now trying to break this dilemma, but it isn't easy to streamline a bureaucracy that is swollen to what some estimate is ten times a truly effective size. To avoid mass unemployment, the government . . . employs some two million people, and in any of the huge state ministry buildings in Cairo one can find large numbers of them just standing around, or, if they are college graduates, sitting in offices at empty desks, trading gossip and reading the newspaper. Those given papers to shuffle find their functions narrow and maddeningly redundant. To prevent this ponderous monster from completely suffocating the interest of investors and the development hopes of the country, a new Foreign Investment Authority has been created to handle all aspects of an investor's application, from licensing construction plans to registering foreign workers. But even with this special attention, notes an American economic official here, it will take at least three years from the time a decision is made to build a plant until the plant can actually begin production. "By then," he adds with discouragement, "you've got another three million people here."

A million new people every year—it is a staggering increase for a country of Egypt's limited size and means, and constitutes the gravest threat of all to its dreams of modernization. Egypt's population has grown from 22 million in 1947 to . . . [around 36] million . . . [in 1975], and if present rates continue unchecked it will reach 70 million by the year 2000. An incredible 40 percent of the present population is younger than fifteen. Public schools and social services are being overwhelmed.

In its 1971 economic plan the government candidly admitted that, if the present rate of increase is not reduced, it "would destroy all hopes of development and progress and, in fact, threaten our very existence." Since 1967 government-sponsored family-planning clinics have been dispensing contraceptives and information in both rural and urban areas; there are . . . almost 4,000 such clinics in the country. An ambitious government population plan announced in 1973 seeks to reduce the growth rate from an official (and inaccurately low) figure of 2 percent . . . [in 1975] to 1.1 percent by 1982, through a multifaceted program stressing not only family-planning services but also the improvement of the standard of living and the status of women, which government planners believe is essential to lowering the birth rate.

While the government is having some success in changing ancient attitudes about birth control and family size, the family-planning programs are riddled with problems, and many feel they are given insufficient priority in government budgets and propaganda. Clinics are understaffed and unevenly distributed. Nurses and doctors are often poorly informed about specific birth control techniques and possible side effects of the contraceptives they dispense. Sex education and birth control are still only barely integrated into the school curricula, while effective mass literature on the subject is hard to come by. And now, incredibly, there is a critical shortage of the commodity on which the whole program rests—the contraceptives themselves.

Enormous problems and enormous potential—that is the story of Egypt . . . [in 1975]. Conversations with the many talented and farsighted leaders in Egyptian government and intellectual life leave one with the feeling that all the giant possibilities and crises of modern development are . . . gathering toward a contest here in this ancient land. And if there is disagreement over strategies and priorities, there is impressive consensus over the need to remove finally that one obstacle which could at any moment shatter all the grand designs of the nation's master planners: the threat of war.

In the halls and offices of Egypt's ministries and newspapers and universities, one hears expressed an aching desire to settle the Middle East crisis once and for all, a fervent hope that Israel might be flexible enough in its negotiating position to enable a permanent peace to emerge, so that the full human and financial energy available to Egypt could at last be turned toward the massive test of its development capacities that is now taking shape.

It was a surprisingly widespread sentiment Osman Ahmed Osman was voicing when he confided recently: "We have nothing against Israel if they will only return our land and grant the Palestinians their rights. Why do you think we are developing our canal zone as we are? We don't want to fight. We are looking for peace."

IRAQ, SAUDI ARABIA, KUWAIT, AND THE MINISTATES [4]

An accident of geology and an appetite for energy have made the Persian Gulf a focus of worldwide interest. Not so long ago the economic activity of this 550-mile-long inlet of the Indian Ocean was confined to pearl fishing, slave trading, piracy and the construction of dhows (Arab sailing boats). The gulf was of strategic interest only because it bordered the shipping lanes to British India. This had led nineteenth century Britain to appoint itself the military and political guardian of the area—a role not formally relinquished until the end of 1971. By then, of course, the gulf's importance as a producer of oil (which was first discovered in Iran in 1908) was clearly established. But it is only . . . [since the early 1970s] that the power of the oil-producing states has clearly emerged. It has been dramatized by the energy crisis in the industrialized world; by the Arabs' successful use of the oil embargo weapon during the October 1973 Arab-Israeli war; by the quadrupling of prices charged to oil customers; and by the multibillion-dollar revenues accruing to oil exporters.

[4] From "The Oil States of the Persian Gulf," chapter no 7 in *Great Decisions 1975*. Foreign Policy Association. '75. p 71-2+. Reprinted by permission. Copyright, 1975 by Foreign Policy Association, Inc. 345 E. 46th St. New York 10017.

Supply and Demand

The . . . countries bordering the Persian Gulf do not account for all "Middle East" oil (Syria and Turkey are small producers) or for all "Arab" oil (in North Africa, Libya is a major producer, Algeria is middling, Egypt and Tunisia are minor). Nor, as of 1973, did any one of the gulf states match the output levels of the world's two biggest oil producers, the United States and the Soviet Union. But the *combined* output . . . for that year, in excess of 20 million barrels a day, represented 35 percent of total world production and 60 percent of the oil moving in world trade.

As of the end of 1973 the . . . gulf producers were believed to possess 55 percent of the world's oil reserves (66 percent of the non-Communist world's). But new estimates published in 1974 more than tripled the earlier figures on Saudi Arabia's "proved" reserves. . . . [In 1975] it appears, that country alone may possess as much as 460 billion barrels—close to half of all the known petroleum on earth.

In 1973 . . . oil supplied 48 percent of the world's energy consumption. The three biggest oil consumers, the United States, Western Europe and Japan, together accounted for 38 million barrels a day, about two thirds of the world total. Proportionately, Japan's dependence was heaviest. Oil supplied 80 percent of all Japanese energy requirements; virtually 100 percent of this oil (5.4 million barrels a day) had to be imported; and 76 percent of the imports came from the Persian Gulf. Roughly 64 percent of Western Europe's energy needs were met by oil; nearly all of the 15.2 million barrels a day it burned were imported; and 68 percent of the imports were of Persian Gulf origin. The United States was the biggest oil consumer, but the 16.8 million barrels a day we burned represented only 47 percent of our total energy consumption. We imported close to 37 percent of our oil in 1973, but the bulk came from the Carribbean and Canadian sources. . . .

Iraq: Socialist Maverick

Besides being the most populous (10.5 million) of the Arab oil states on the Persian Gulf, Iraq has several other distinctions. It is the site of what the ancients called Meso-potamia, the "land between the rivers" (the Tigris and Euphrates), where the world's oldest known civilization was born more than five thousand years ago. . . . [In 1975] it is the only gulf nation not ruled by a hereditary monarch. It is the only regime professing (if not always practicing) a "radical" ideology. It is the one on warmest terms with the Soviet Union and coolest terms with the United States. In many observers' judgment, it is the least stable internally.

Army officers toppled the Iraqi monarchy in a 1957 coup. Since then, various military factions have been running the country. A faction adhering to the Baath (Arab Socialist Renaissance) party, which also governs Syria, has been in power since 1968. The Iraqi Baathists, under the leadership of Major General Ahmad Hassan al-Bakr—who serves as both president and prime minister—have reached a shaky political truce with their bitterest rivals, the Communists. They have welcomed large inputs of Soviet military and economic aid, including development of the important new North Rumeila oil field (in southern Iraq), and in April 1972 they signed a fifteen-year treaty of friendship and co-operation with Moscow.

But the Baghdad leaders are also interested in a steady, profitable market in the West for their oil. They took a major step to secure this early in 1973, when they agreed on terms of compensation for the nationalized Iraq Petroleum Company with the former Western owners. Official Bagh-dad-Washington relations, broken off during the June 1967 Arab-Israeli war, have yet [in 1975] to be fully restored. But the two governments maintain low-level diplomatic repre-sentation, and private business activity has been little af-fected. . . .

In 1973 Iraq was the fourth biggest oil producer in the Middle East. Like Iran, it could apply the bulk of its oil profits to domestic development. Thanks to the two historic rivers, about a third of the land is suitable for farming, grazing or forestry. Most Iraqis live by agriculture, raising dates, grain, livestock, cotton and other crops.

By far the gravest problem plaguing the Iraqi rulers is the Kurdish minority. The Kurds are a tribal people ethnically akin to the Iranians. As many as two million of them—a fifth of the entire population—live in the northern and the eastern regions of the country. For years they have been demanding, and sporadically fighting for, an autonomous province of their own, one that would not be dominated by the Arab majority in the rest of the country. The main obstacle to a negotiated accord has been the oil-producing centers of Kirkuk and Mosul in northern Iraq. Baghdad refuses to relinquish control over these strategic areas, whereas the Kurdish leader, General Mustafa al-Barzani, insists that they be included in a self-governing Kurdistan.

Saudi Arabia: Custodian of Tradition

There are no minority problems in the desert kingdom where the Arab people originated and the prophet Mohammed was born. Saudi Arabia is a homogeneous and highly traditional society—tribal, feudal and theocratic. Its [late] sixty-nine-year-old ruler, King Faisal [who was assassinated in 1975], . . . [was] the official custodian of the holiest places of Islam (the cities of Mecca and Medina in Saudi Arabia and the Dome of the Rock in Jerusalem) and . . . [was] a devout adherent of . . . [a] puritanical . . . sect. He also . . . [presided] over the world's richest reservoir of oil, which is belatedly propelling his country into the mainstream of twentieth century life. Faisal's goal, as one observer summarizes it, . . . [was] "to lead his people to universal prosperity while insulating them from the mischief of socialism, the godlessness of communism and the decadence of the liberal democracies." [Since the death of Faisal, King Khalid has ruled Saudi Arabia.—Ed.]

Saudi Arabia has no constitution, no parliament. The

nation is administered by the two thousand royal princes of
the Saud clan. They are all related to Abdul-Aziz ibn Saud,
a Bedouin warlord who welded the modern kingdom together
between 1902 and 1932 through a series of military conquests and marriages. . . . The law of the land is the Koran.
Slavery has been banned only since 1962. Women are still
forbidden to drive cars and to hold jobs that bring them
into contact with men, and most still wear the veil in public.

But the winds of change are stirring, very gently but unmistakably, through this rigidly conservative society. When
television was introduced to Saudi Arabia . . . [in 1965], even
Minnie Mouse was barred from the screen because she was
female. . . . [In 1975] foreign women can appear on TV if
they are chastely clad, and Saudi girls are attending universities. The new technocrat class, comprising around 3,500
Saudis who have been trained at American and other foreign universities, is in huge demand for top managerial and
engineering jobs. The middle class of merchants, manufacturers and bankers is fast expanding. A generation ago the
commercial center of Jidda on the Red Sea and the royal
capital of Riyadh in the central Nejd desert were little more
than mud-brick townships. . . . [In 1975] they are gleaming
with modern air-conditioned office buildings, hotels, luxury
villas and supermarkets. Across the huge, sparsely populated
country a modern infrastructure is steadily being laid down:
roads, airports, harbors, oil refineries, schools, hospitals,
clinics.

Using about $5 billion a year from its oil earnings, the
Saudi government aims to create a welfare state on a par
with Kuwait; to equip its armed forces with the most up-to-
date weapons; to develop the country's agricultural and
mineral resources and a diversified industrial base. Besides
oil and gas, the Saudi Arabian subsoil is rich in tin, copper,
aluminum, zinc, iron ore, silver, gold and uranium. The
Saudis envisage steel mills, auto assembly plants, petrochemical industries, etc. in the future "postoil" age. In the
shorter run, they are eager to develop a chemical-fertilizer

industry that will use some of the 5 billion cubic feet a day of natural gas that are now being wastefully burned off Saudi oil wells.

For all these ambitious development plans, as well as for guidance on investing the billions they will still have left over, the Saudis welcome foreign advice. And as one observer notes drily, "the number of eminent Western bankers offering them expertise is approaching mob proportions." Of all the Westerners in evidence, Americans are the most conspicuous. A "special relationship" between the two countries dates back to the early post-World War II years when the United States responded to Saudi requests for military and technical assistance. In addition to being the principal concessionaires for Saudi Arabia's oil industry through the consortium of four US companies known as Aramco, Americans have long been its leading suppliers of military equipment. An American air base at Dhahran from 1952 to 1962 was closed down partly because of Saudi displeasure at US aid to Israel. Washington's pro-Israel policy has, in fact, been the only serious blemish on Saudi-American friendship, and now this seems to have been smoothed over at least temporarily by Secretary of State Kissinger's Mideast diplomacy. . . .

[In 1974] the two governments signed a wide-ranging agreement on economic and security matters that, they said, "heralded an era of increasingly close cooperation." Nowhere in the text of the accord was the word "oil" mentioned. But US officials made no secret of their hope that the Saudis, who . . . own a controlling interest in Aramco [Arabian American Oil Company], will see fit to step up their oil production.

Kuwait: Welfare State

Oil production in Kuwait, the gulf's third-biggest producer after Saudi Arabia and Iran, has been cut back to less than three million barrels a day to stretch the life of reserves. This little desert country the size of Connecticut and

Rhode Island combined, with fewer than a million inhabitants, hardly needs to boost oil sales. Its per capita wealth was on a par with that of the United States, Sweden or Switzerland until . . . [1974], when it soared above $8,000 (the US level is around $6,000).

Kuwait is already the very model of a modern welfare state, with womb-to-tomb security assured for all citizens. All education and health care are free, and the government will pay the expenses of any Kuwaiti going abroad for university study or medical treatment. Telephone service is free. Taxes are nonexistent except for import duties. Every Kuwaiti is guaranteed a job—in the civil service if no one else will have him—and cannot be fired without the personal authorization of the crown prince. One in every three Kuwaitis owns a car. "The only thing left to be done," quips one foreign resident, "is to enclose the entire country under an air-conditioned dome."

Kuwait is a tolerant and cosmopolitan society. For centuries the port city was a trading center, and its influential merchant families have been more exposed to new ideas and customs than the desert Bedouins in the interior of the peninsula. It was also a British protectorate until 1961 and, outside of Lebanon, has the closest thing to a parliamentary regime in the Arab world. Kuwait is not quite a democracy, since neither the figurehead emir nor Crown Prince Jaber al-Ahmad al-Jaber (who also serves as prime minister) is accountable to the legislature. But other government officials are, and the parliamentary opposition is vigorous. Kuwait also has a relatively free press and independent trade unions. Social attitudes are relatively enlightened. Women have not worn the veil since 1956, hold jobs and are soon expected to win the vote. Alcohol is technically illegal in Moslem Kuwait, but anyone who wants a drink can find one.

Another Koranic taboo, on usury (the collection of interest on money loaned), is increasingly ignored. Kuwait has become a major center of world finance. It is now the fourth-biggest underwriter of the World Bank and the headquarters for development aid to the poorer Arab and Islamic nations. The Kuwait Investment Company, half owned by the government and half by private citizens, has real estate holdings extending from Paris to Atlanta . . . and has floated bond issues in Finland and Canada and Brazil.

About the only cloud on Kuwait's sunny horizon is the fact that more than half of its 900,000 inhabitants are foreigners: Palestinians, Egyptians, Lebanese, Iranians, Pakistanis, Yemenis, etc. Their services, ranging from the highest professional skills to the most menial labor, are sorely needed. But the discrimination against them as noncitizens —they may not own property, share fully in the welfare-state benefits or qualify for as high salaries as Kuwaitis earn—is a sore point that could worsen with time.

The Ministates

Of the . . . remaining states bordering the Persian Gulf, three are minor oil producers. The sheikdom of Bahrein, an archipelago of thirty-three tiny coral islands, was the first to discover oil (in 1932) and will probably be the first to run dry. Qatar, a dry little peninsula, has only as much territory as Kuwait with not a tenth of its oil resources. The Sultanate of Oman (formerly called Muscat and Oman) possesses even less oil, but it has two features of interest. A strip of Omani territory commands the Arabian shore of the strategically important Strait of Hormuz, the narrow neck of the Persian Gulf through which all oceangoing tankers must pass. And the southernmost province of Oman, Dhofar, is the site of a Marxist guerrilla insurgency; if the rebels win, they could eventually dominate the approaches to the gulf along the entire Arabian coast.

The fourth gulf ministate, United Arab Emirates (UAE), is a loose federation of seven sheikdoms, formerly called the Trucial States, on what used to be known as the Pirate Coast of the Arabian peninsula. To date three of the emirates, Abu Dhabi, Dubai and Sharjah, have found oil. But the only significant producer is Abu Dhabi. It is the capital of UAE and accounts for 90 percent of the federation's territory, more than three quarters of its oil and half of its population. Abu Dhabi's per capita income is far and away the world's highest. . . . [In 1974] it shot up to the staggering sum of $40,000 for each of the 110,000 inhabitants.

The town of Abu Dhabi, a mud-brick fishing village when oil was first discovered in 1958, is . . . [in 1975] a case study in the chaos of instant development. It has stately new boulevards on the Parisian scale, a sumptuous guest palace with gold ceilings and marble coffee tables, hovels slapped together for the swarms of immigrant laborers, spanking new high-rise buildings that are already beginning to crumble because foreign contractors have taken a shortcut to overnight profits by mixing their cement with seawater. Sheik Zaid bin Sultan al-Nihyan, the ruler of Abu Dhabi and president of the UAE is a Bedouin chief with no formal schooling whose favorite pastime is hunting with falcons in the desert. But he has imported planeloads of foreign technical experts and financial advisers at top salaries to help manage Abu Dhabi's booming fortunes—a far cry from the days of his father, who hoarded the shiekdom's assets in the form of gold bars stacked under his bed.

Among the recent foreign arrivals in Abu Dhabi is an American ambassador to the UAE. Washington's diplomatic representation in the federation, Oman, Bahrein and Qatar used to be through the US envoy in Kuwait. . . . [In 1975] all four gulf ministates have been upgraded to the level of embassies with resident ambassadors. It is yet another sign of the region's growing status on the world scene.

ARAB OIL MONEY BACKS SUDAN'S DEVELOPMENT [5]

In the late nineteenth century, an Englishman described Sudan this way:

[5] From "Arab Oil Money Backs Sudan's Development as Prime Food Source," by Ray Vicker, staff reporter. *Wall Street Journal.* p 1+. N. 24, '75. Reprinted with permission of *The Wall Street Journal* © 1975 Dow Jones & Company, Inc. All rights reserved.

For godforsaken, dry-sucked, fly-blown wilderness, commend me to the Upper Nile, a desolation of desolations, an infernal region, a howling waste of weed, mosquitoes, flies and fever. I have passed through it, and now have no fear of the hereafter.

A British war correspondent in the same period said of Sudan: "Nothing grows green. For beasts it has tarantulas and scorpions and serpents, devouring white ants, and every kind of loathsome bug that flies or crawls."

Even the Sudanese coined a bitter proverb about their land: "When Allah made Sudan, Allah laughed."

Paradoxically, this much maligned land now is viewed as the potential food basket of the Middle East. This is no empty dream, either. Arab oil money for agricultural development is already pouring in.

The heat, the scorpions and the bugs are still here, and northern Sudan does contain some of the bleakest deserts on earth, but the central and southern regions have enormous tracts of rich land, and adequate rainfall. Moreover, the White Nile surges northward across Sudan from Central Africa, and the Blue Nile flows up from Ethiopia; both could be tapped more for irrigation.

In a Worried World

"This country has a tremendous potential in agriculture," says Daffaala Hag Yusif, managing director . . . [in Sudan] for Gulf Interational, the big Kuwaiti conglomerate. "The Sudan," he adds, "has 200 million acres of good land, and only 17 million acres are being used. Consider what that means in a world that is becoming ever more worried about its food supplies."

Among those worrying most are oil-rich countries. While Westerners fear another oil embargo if political troubles develop in the Middle East, Arabs fear that any such embargo could cause food problems for them; Saudi Arabia, Kuwait, Abu Dhabi and most other Arab oil lands must import much of their food. So as the Ford Administration seeks to reduce the United States' oil dependency on the Middle East, oil producers are trying to reduce their food dependency on the United States and other Western nations.

In this quest, they are focusing increasingly on Sudan, a black, basically Moslem and Arab country that is aligned with the Arab League and other Arab groups. "All the Arab oil-producing countries are giving us help," says Hussein Idris, Sudan's minister of state for agriculture. "Some of these countries are afraid that, even with all their money, they may have trouble obtaining food supplies in the future from outside this area. Investments in Sudan are assuring those supplies at prices cheaper than from anywhere else."

Results Apparent

The happy combination of good land, Arab money and foreign technology is already producing results: Within a few years [from 1975] Sudan, now a sugar importer, is scheduled to become an exporter of over 700,000 metric tons of cane sugar a year; experiments have proved the feasibility of flying fruits and vegetables to European and Middle Eastern markets; the output of grains such as rice and sorghum is climbing; Sudan is expected to become a major meat exporter.

According to preliminary estimates, total production of nine major crops in Sudan in 1974-1975 was about 28 percent above the level of the preceding year. Transport and port facilities are being overhauled to handle a much larger volume.

The Arab Fund for Social and Economic Development, which is financed to a large extent with oil money, has outlined a hundred long-range projects that could further stimulate farming here. Minister Idris estimates that these would require investment of $5.5 billion.

Sudan's net capital inflow was a meager $3 million in 1973. In 1974, it was $227 million. "The bulk of that inflow," says Mohamed el Kheir Abdel Gadir, acting director general of the National Planning Commission, "came from the Arab oil-producing countries." Kuwait alone accounted for $93.5 million.

Continent's Biggest Country

In area, Sudan is Africa's largest country. It stretches for 967,500 square miles along the Red Sea and south from Libya and Egypt to Uganda. In the north, the desert rolls back from both sides of the Nile. Even solitary blades of grass have trouble taking root in the endless dunes. Only a handful of nomads eke out a living from flocks of gaunt goats and camels. In this area not far from the Red Sea, a Bisharin tribesman hugs the shelter of a thorn tree in 125-degree heat. These tribesmen, "fuzzy wuzzies" to [Rudyard] Kipling, are the originators of the Afro hairdo. They are independent, sometimes belligerently so, and are able to survive where even scorpions battle for existence.

The fuzzy wuzzy and his arid region provided Europe with its first and most lasting impression of this country. There is no doubt, however, that the entire country is poor; the United Nations places Sudan, with its annual income of $125 per capita, among the fifteen least-developed countries in the world.

In the south, the White Nile spreads into a vast swamp, the Sudd. Roads are waterlogged for six months of the year. At one pool, several crocodiles sun themselves on a mud bank, slithering into the muddy water when disturbed. Somewhere, amid tall green strands of papyrus, a hippo grunts quarrelsomely.

But between northern desert and southern swamp lies mile after mile of savanna country. This is grassland—somewhat like the plains of Nebraska and the Dakotas, though flatter. Near Wad Medani, south of . . . [Khartoum], fields of cotton stretch on and on. Cotton, the long-staple variety highly valued by textile mills, is a key farm product and a key foreign currency earner. Each year, Sudan produces 1 million to 1.2 million bales on about 1.2 million acres of cotton land. Further south, below the cotton fields, fat cattle and sheep graze beside the Blue Nile.

If a farmer in this region has irrigation, he and his fam-

ily thrive. Idris Dafalla, who lives near Barakat . . . , wipes
his hands on his long white gown after opening an irrigation channel to shunt Blue Nile water onto some of his ten
acres. Then, pulling at his goatee, he talks about his five
acres of cotton and his crop of peanuts, his wheat and his
vegetables.

Subsistence Plus

At forty-nine, Mr. Dafalla supports his wife, eleven children, his mother and mother-in-law on a farm that offers
subsistence plus $1,700 a year. That is way above the coun-
try's average, and he considers himself well enough off to
buy some luxuries. "I have the bride money," he says. "I am
thinking of finding me a second wife." She would move in
with the first wife and the rest of the family.

The two Niles join . . . at Khartoum, forming the main
Nile. Then their waters run side by side for another twenty
to thirty miles before thoroughly mixing on the journey to
the north. . . . [During the fall season], with summer rains
still draining from the Ethiopian highlands, the Blue Nile
is more light brown than blue, while the white of the White
Nile is that of heavily creamed coffee. On the peninsula
where the rivers join, a Hilton hotel is under construction, a
new building symbolizing the new spirit in this country of
many projects.

Six-Million-Acre Project

Four projects are being studied by the Arab Organization for Agricultural Development, an Arab League affiliate
with headquarters here, says the organization's director general, Kamal Ramzy Stino. The biggest of the four would involve 6 million acres of fertile, largely unused land along
the Blue Nile. A $75 million program would bring a million
of these acres into cattle production as a starter.

Triad Natural Resources (Sudan) Ltd., a key company

of the Saudi Arabian financier Adnan Khashoggi, is launching another cattle development project in the same area. A range would be established on 1.2 million acres of generally undeveloped land at a cost of $93 million. AZL International Corporation, a subsidiary of Arizona-Colorado Land & Cattle Company, would manage the operation. The range would handle 68,000 cattle and 18,000 sheep.

Agricultural specialists believe that livestock is particularly suitable for development here. Sudan already has an estimated 40 million head of animals—14 million cattle, 13 million sheep, 10 million goats and 3 million camels. But the animals are generally raised in haphazard fashion by nomads and farmers who sometimes measure their wealth in cattle numbers, not quality. It is recognized that quality must be raised to expand export markets.

"To make better use of this potential, the government has established several projects for the development of animal production, including measures for combating diseases and for the establishment of a disease-free zone, and the construction of appropriate slaughterhouses that meet with international specifications and standards," says Major Abu el Gasim Mohamed Ibrahim, minister of agriculture, food and natural resources.

The biggest government project under way is an irrigation project at Rahad. This $240 million project, aided by Kuwait and Saudi Arabia, will bring water from the Blue Nile to 300,000 acres through a 50-mile-long canal. The land will be planted mainly in cotton and peanuts, with 20,000 acres to be devoted to fruits and vegetables.

Several sugar estates and refineries are being brought into production. At Kenana, 300,000 acres are being developed for production of 300,000 metric tons of sugar annually by the end of this decade. Britain's Lonrho Group, a big conglomerate, is managing the project and holds a 10 percent interest. (It is estimated that a quarter of all Lonrho equity now is held by Arabs of the Persian Gulf.)

Sudan will produce about 175,000 tons of sugar in the fiscal year ending . . . June 30 [1976] while consuming 320,000 tons. The aim is to raise output to 1.2 million tons in 1980, with 430,000 tons for local consumption and 775,000 for export.

IV. THE ARABS AND ISRAEL

EDITOR'S INTRODUCTION

The Middle East has seen four wars between the Arab countries and Israel within the last thirty years. Despite decades of peacekeeping efforts by the United Nations, and by third-party governments, there was little movement toward a settlement. In fact, no Arab country will negotiate directly with Israel, nor would Israel conduct talks with Palestinian guerrillas until March 1976, when unrest in Israeli-occupied territory created new tensions. So deep are the enmities and suspicions that a solution often seems impossible.

In 1974, and again in 1975, Israel agreed to limited withdrawals from occupied Egyptian land. This raised hopes that agreements could also be reached with Jordan and Syria, Israel's other principal antagonists, and that the wheels could be set in motion for a Middle East settlement. However, in 1974, the United Nations gave permanent observer status to the Palestine Liberation Organization (PLO), the armed group that represents Arabs whose original homeland is now within Israel. In 1975 the UN invited the PLO to participate in its debate on the Middle East. Then the General Assembly voted to condemn Zionism—the movement calling for the return of the Jewish people to Israel—as a form of racism. These actions infuriated Israel because they seemed to legitimize a terrorist organization and because, in Israel's view, the world body had succumbed to the pressure of Arab oil power in equating Zionism and Israel with racism.

This section explores the issues in the Arab-Israeli conflict. The first article reviews recent events and discusses the role of the United States as mediator in trying to bring the two sides together. The second article looks at the recent political successes of the Palestine Liberation Organization and at the Israeli reaction to these successes. The next article, by reporter Henry Tanner of the New York *Times*, exposes the deep divisions within the Arab world over the various approaches to dealing with Israel. This article details how the limited agreement between Israel and Egypt has provoked sharp disagreement among Arab governments.

The final article in this section recounts a conversation between an Arab and an Israeli. It suggests that despite the bitterness between the two sides a solution is possible—if only the two sides would agree to discuss their differences at the negotiating table.

ARABS VERSUS ISRAELIS [1]

"A pause, not a peace" is how Senator George McGovern (Democrat, South Dakota) described . . . [the September 1975] Sinai accord between Israel and Egypt. Few expected the interim agreement on partial military disengagement to do more than buy time for achieving a comprehensive Middle East peace settlement.

This was the second limited pullback of Israeli forces on Egypt's Sinai peninsula agreed upon since the October 1973 Arab-Israeli war. Like the first accord in January 1974, it owed much to the vigorous mediation efforts of US Secretary of State Henry A. Kissinger. But this time Kissinger's celebrated "shuttle diplomacy" between . . . [Israeli Prime Minister] Yitzhak Rabin's government in Jerusalem and [Egyptian] President Anwar Sadat's summer headquarters in Alexandria climaxed many weeks of hard bargaining behind the scenes.

Sinai: Who Gets What

Israel's key concessions to Egypt in the Sinai package are two strategically situated mountain passes, Mitla and Gidi, and the Abu Rudeis oil fields farther south. (The latter have supplied more than half of Israel's petroleum needs since

[1] From chapter no 1 of *Great Decisions 1976*. Foreign Policy Association. '76. p 1-7. Reprinted by permission. Copyright, 1976 by Foreign Policy Association, Inc. 345 E. 46th St. New York 10017.

they were occupied in the June 1967 war.) In all, Egypt is
recovering some two thousand square miles of the huge,
sparsely populated peninsula; Israel still controls more than
85 percent of it.

Besides the Abu Rudeis oil and the assurance that traffic
on the Suez Canal—reopened in June 1975—will now be
safely out of Israeli artillery range, the Egyptians can look
forward to material benefits from abroad. The Ford Administration is asking Congress to approve more than a half-
billion dollars' worth of economic aid to Egypt and is considering the future sale to Cairo of jet fighter aircraft and
antitank missiles. Sadat is further counting on an upsurge
of private business investment from American and other
Western sources.

Israel's principal gains from the Sinai deal are twofold:
conciliatory political gestures by Egypt and the pledge of a
hefty aid package from the United States. Egypt has joined
Israel in a written commitment to resolve their conflict by
peaceful means and not to resort to the use or threat of force
for the duration of the new accord. Both governments have
publicly hailed the accord as "a significant step toward a
just and lasting peace." Egypt will permit nonmilitary cargoes bound to and from Israel in third country ships to
transit the Suez Canal. It has undertaken to extend the mandate of the UN [United Nations] peacekeeping force in
Sinai for a full year at a time and to renew it at least twice.
Egypt intends to see that the government controlled news
media tone down their anti-Israel propaganda, that the
Egyptian embargo on American companies doing business
with Israel is at least partly eased and that Cairo does not
actively discourage other nations from resuming diplomatic
relations with Jerusalem. (This last applies most particularly
to some African countries which broke ties with Israel after
the October 1973 war.)

The Ford Administration, for its part, promised the
Rabin government in a separate bilateral understanding to
ask Congress for up to $2.3 billion worth of aid in the . . .
1976 fiscal year alone. The military portion would cover

fighter-bomber and interceptor aircraft, ground-to-ground missiles and laser-guided "smart" bombs. Much of the economic portion would compensate the Israelis for the loss of the Abu Rudeis oil fields, with $350 million or so toward their added costs of buying oil on the world market. Moreover, if they are unable to obtain all they need from Iran and other sources, the United States itself "will promptly make oil available for purchase by Israel."

The most publicized American contribution, however, is the stationing of American observers in the Sinai. Up to two hundred civilian technicians, recruited and paid by the US government, will be assigned to the area of the Mitla and Gidi passes. They will help to monitor one Israeli and one Egyptian early warning facility and will independently manage a half-dozen smaller posts. The introduction of an American peacekeeping presence on the Arab-Israeli front lines has aroused considerable controversy in the United States. But without it, Egypt and Israel were unwilling to accept the accord.

Reactions

In only two capitals, Washington and Cairo, was the Sinai agreement hailed with unalloyed satisfaction. President Gerald R. Ford and Secretary Kissinger were gratified by the latest American diplomatic success in the quest for Mideast peace and the further displacement of Soviet influence in a pivotal Arab country, Egypt. In Cairo, President Sadat was happy to have a respite from military confrontation so that the Egyptians could at last turn their energies to the neglected domestic economy. In Jerusalem, however, the prevailing feeling was no more than lukewarm—"the best we could get under the circumstances," according to one high Israeli official. Washington had very much wanted the Israelis' signature on an agreement. And the latter could refuse only at the price of alienating their best friend and sole arms supplier.

Some other judgments on the Egyptian-Israeli accord

were more severe. Even before it was signed, reported a cor-respondent in Beirut [Lebanon], it was "already an apple of discord in the Arab camp." Sadat did enjoy the diplo-matic backing of oil-rich Saudi Arabia, whose financial back-ing is indispensable to his development plans for Egypt. But his deal with the Israelis was denounced by many of the other Arab leaders—Syrian, Iraqi, Palestinian. Yasir Arafat, head of the Palestine Liberation Organization (PLO), com-plained bitterly that the Sinai pact ignored his people com-pletely: "In fact, it goes out of its way to avoid the heart of the whole Middle Eastern conflict." [See "Sinai Pact Stirs Misgivings Among Arabs," in this section, below.]

By isolating Sadat from his fellow Arabs and detaching Egypt from the confrontation with Israel, said other critics, the Sinai accord removed the most important Arab military power from what should be a concerted effort toward a *com-prehensive* peace. The Washington *Post* concluded that the new agreement "will only be worth celebrating if it is fol-lowed by a swift and serious effort to get on with the job of producing a comprehensive Mideast settlement."

The Administration answered its critics by maintaining that the Sinai accord was the most that realistically could be achieved at this time. But it too agrees on the importance of reaching an overall settlement. By common consent, this is one of the toughest challenges facing the world today. Three distinct aspects of the search for lasting peace in the Middle East are of prime concern to American policy makers. First, are solutions possible to the most fundamental and intract-able points at issue between Arabs and Israelis? What would be the best diplomatic approach to solutions? And finally, what role should the United States play in the whole process?

The Arab-Israeli conflict, as one newspaper editorial summarized it, "has to do at bottom with (1) the right of Israel to exist within secure borders and to coexist in a nor-mal way with its neighbors; (2) the claims of the Palestinians for recognition of their rights to exist in some sort of sovereign state; and (3) the demands of the Arabs for a return of all Israeli-occupied territory." (This last means the territory that Israeli forces conquered from Syria, Jordan and Egypt in the Six-Day War of June 1967.)

Underlying these political-military issues is an even deeper emotional one that complicates the search for solutions. This is the mutual suspicion, if not hatred, rooted in a quarter-century of Arab-Israeli antagonism and four full-scale wars (in 1948-1949, 1956, 1967 and 1973). "The basic difficulty which governs all the others," writes former US Ambassador to the UN Charles W. Yost, "is mistrust. The Israelis for the most part simply do not believe the assertions of Arab leaders that they are prepared to accept the existence of Israel within the 1967 lines. . . . The Arabs, for their part, do not believe Israel will evacuate the territories seized in 1967 unless forced to do so either by great-power pressure or by war." An Israeli politician . . . has put it another way: The Israelis are haunted by fears of annihilation while the Arabs are haunted by fears of unbridled Israeli expansionism.

Are the Arabs Ready to Coexist With Israel?

In 1948 there was no question that the new Jewish state created by the UN's partition of Palestine was intolerable to its Arab neighbors. In 1976 there is still considerable question whether Israel's neighbors are at last ready to tolerate its existence—at least within its pre-June 1967 frontiers.

A growing body of opinion contends that they are. "Gone are the days of [Gamal Abdel] Nasser's period," King Khalid of Saudi Arabia assured a visiting American legislator, "when the Arabs threatened to exterminate the Israelis." According to J. William Fulbright, former chairman of the Senate Foreign Relations Committee, the leaders of the principal Arab countries . . . [in 1976]—Khalid of Saudi Arabia, Sadat of Egypt, King Hussein of Jordan, President Hafez Assad of Syria—are "moderate and responsible" men who are "united in a consensus for making peace with Israel on the basis of the 1967 borders. All of them say so, explicitly and without qualification," adds Fulbright, "and the head of the PLO, Yasir Arafat, says so too, guardedly and by indirection, but, to my ear, unmistakably." . . .

Many who share this view warn, however, that the opportunity to make peace may not last long. If the Israelis continue to plead Arab "nonacceptance" of Israel as a pretext not to budge from the occupied territories, they say, then the Arab moderates . . . holding power will inevitably be replaced by more militant leaders. For example, Arafat could be supplanted by the radical Marxist [Dr.] George Habash, leader of the so-called Rejection Front of the PLO.

But a substantial school of opinion holds the opposite view—that the Arabs are *not* prepared to accept more than a temporary truce with Israel. "There is no reason to believe that the PLO or Syria, or even in the longer run, Egypt, will be satisfied by any particular set of concessions," writes Amitai Etzioni, an Israeli scholar living in the United States. "The sad reality just may be that the Israeli-Arab conflict is not currently amenable to solution. . . . Ultimately the Arabs are not ready to live in peace with a viable Israel." Of supreme importance to Israelis is what they call the "nature of peace." This means solid evidence that the Arabs are reconciled to permanent, normal coexistence: an end to economic boycotts and hostile propaganda, a free flow of trade, tourism, cultural exchanges, diplomatic recognition. The Israelis, it is argued, cannot reasonably be asked to give up something tangible—territory—in exchange for vague rhetorical assurances of peaceful relations "in the next generation" (Sadat's words). They must insist on secure, defensible borders as well as explicit, binding, durable commitments from their Arab neighbors. And, aware that those commitments could be repudiated by new "revolutionary" Arab regimes, they also need military assurances of Israel's ability to survive—demilitarized buffer zones, an ample supply of arms, and so on.

Further, goes the argument, even the "moderate" Palestinians (as opposed to the Rejectionists or the lunatic-fringe terrorists disowned by the PLO) remain dedicated to the dismantling of Israel. Lasting peace, Arafat reiterated in . . . [an] interview, requires that "the state called Israel integrate itself in the region" and give way to "a modern, democratic, secular state in which Jews, Moslems and Christians would live side by side on the basis of full equality." Even if we take Arafat at his word that this would not mean the destruction of the Jewish *people*—to whom he offers a "historic opportunity" to "partake in the development of the entire region"—he plainly envisages the destruction of the Jewish *state* over the long term.

For the shorter term, the more moderate PLO leaders are apparently ready to accept a compromise arrangement: a Palestinian ministate alongside of Israel.

What Would Be a "Just" Solution for the Palestinians?

One of the basic principles of an Arab-Israeli peace settlement set forth in the UN Security Council's landmark Resolution 242, adopted unanimously on November 22, 1967, is the need to achieve a "just settlement of the refugee problem." The wording was deliberately made vague enough so that all parties to the dispute could endorse the resolution. (Israel, Egypt, and Jordan did; Syria did not.) In the view of many analysts, the problem of the refugees—Palestinian Arabs displaced from their ancestral homeland by Israel's victories in the 1948-1949 war—is the very heart of the whole matter.

There are some 3.5 million Palestinians scattered throughout the Middle East today. Most are Moslem, a few are Christian. Half still live in what used to be Palestine: the state of Israel proper plus Israeli-occupied East Jerusalem and the [Jordan River's] West Bank (both of which were ruled by Jordan until the 1967 war) and the Gaza Strip. The remaining Palestinians are exiles. Thousands live in UN-subsidized refugee camps. The rest have found homes in neighboring countries, particularly in Jordan (the only country where they enjoy full citizenship rights), Lebanon, Syria, Kuwait and other Persian Gulf states.

The PLO, now headquartered in Damascus [Syria], was founded in 1964 as an umbrella organization to coordinate the various factions of Palestinian commandos (the *fedayeen*, "men who sacrifice themselves"). Chairman Arafat, who doubles as chief of the biggest commando faction, Al Fatah ("Victory"), is behaving more and more like the leader of a government-in-exile. He was invited to address the UN in November 1974. At that point the General Assembly, which had already recognized the PLO as "the representative of the Palestinian people," passed two further resolutions. The first affirmed the Palestinians' right to self-determination and sovereign independence. The second granted observer status in UN affairs to the PLO; since then, Palestinian delegations have attended a number of international conferences.

The US government voted against all three of these resolutions. Nevertheless, as a New York *Times* editorial has put it, "Political self-expression for the Palestinian population is emerging for all sides as a legitimate cause, however much disagreement remains on how that self-expression should be institutionalized."

What, then, would constitute a "just" solution?

☐ *Choice of repatriation or compensation?* The formula originally voted in December 1948 by the UN General Assembly has never been repealed. It offered the Palestinian refugees the right to choose between returning to their homes to live in peace with their Israeli neighbors or receiving financial compensation for their lost or damaged property. But Israel has always opposed readmitting more than a token number of refugees on the grounds that the repatriated Arabs would not only constitute a security problem but, with their much higher birthrate, would soon outnumber Israel's Jews and alter the character of the country.

Israeli officials have on occasion spoken in very general terms of compensation to Palestinians or contribution to a resettlement fund.

☐ *Permanent resettlement in surrounding Arab countries?* This is the longstanding formula of the Israeli government—that the Arabs who rejected the 1948 partition of Palestine and launched the war against the infant state of Israel are properly responsible for the refugees and should absorb them. In practice, thousands of Palestinian Arabs—the educated elite whose commercial, financial and professional skills are in great demand—have found rewarding careers and comfortable lives in other Arab countries. But no Arab country is willing to support a mass of indigent refugees. And even the affluent minority professes to want the option, at least, of national self-determination. "Lebanon has been kind to me, but Palestine is my country," says one wealthy insurance executive in Beirut. "What is important," insists a Palestinian who teaches business administration at . . . American University in the same city, "is the question of free choice, both for Palestinians and Israeli Jews. Israel denies this today."

☐ *A ministate on Jordan's West Bank and the Gaza Strip?* Palestinian Arabs already comprise virtually the entire population of these two Israeli-occupied areas. The idea of a mini-Palestine, fully independent or loosely federated with Jordan, has been gaining currency throughout the Arab world. Palestinians who are not militant extremists see it as a feasible compromise which would at least provide them with the basic attributes of national sovereignty: their own territory, flag and passport.

The Israeli government and, according to polls, a majority of Israeli citizens are . . . firmly opposed to the establishment of a sovereign Palestinian state. But a number of Israeli "doves" in the political opposition or private life are more tolerant of the idea. Some have openly endorsed it—on the all-important condition that a Palestinian government be headed by responsible moderates, not militant guerrillas.

One new left-of-center Israeli political party formed . . . [in spring 1975] calls for recognition of the PLO, *provided* that the latter first acknowledges Israel's sovereignty and ceases all acts of terror against it. Palestinian leaders, for their part, do not exclude the implicit recognition of Israel *provided* that the latter first recognizes the PLO.

☐ *A reunited "secular" Palestine?* A West Bank-Gaza mini-state, as the Palestinians see it, would be only a step leading in "10, 50 or 100 years" to the fulfillment of their ultimate vision. This would essentially be a restoration of the geographic entity that Britain ruled under a League of Nations mandate from 1923 to 1948. (For several centuries until World War I Palestine had been part of the Turkish empire; in November 1947 the UN General Assembly voted to divide the mandated territory into Arab and Jewish states.) A reunited Palestine—the "modern, democratic, secular state" cited by Arafat and his colleagues—would by definition bar a regime by any one religious group. To the Israelis, as we have noted, it would mean the dismemberment of their nation and society.

What Should Become of the Occupied Territories?

The same UN resolution that calls for a "just" Palestinian solution prescribes two other key steps: (1) "Withdrawal of Israeli armed forces from territories of recent conflict" and (2) ". . . acknowledgment of the sovereignty, territorial integrity and political independence of every state in the area and their right to live in peace within secure and recognized boundaries. . . ." What this translates to is a *quid pro quo:* return of the occupied lands by Israel in exchange for Arab agreement to live in peace with Israel.

Israel has relinquished a few strips of territory, and a few Arab leaders have signaled their acceptance of Israel as a fact of Middle East life. But no more. To the Arabs, Israel's continued rule over the lands seized in the [1967] Six-Day War represents an intolerable foreign military occupation. To the Israelis it represents an indispensable margin of safety from attack in the absence of real peace. Yet the five occupied areas are quite different from each other. Some appear more susceptible to compromise than others:

☐ *Sinai.* The Israeli government has never disputed the fact that this vast peninsula is Egyptian territory. But it is reluctant to pull out of the desert buffer zone without some assurance that, after it did, there would be enough time to mobilize Israel's defenses against a surprise overland invasion. One possibility is the demilitarization of Sinai under UN auspices. But Sharm-el-Sheikh at the southern tip of the peninsula is a special case. This strategic outpost guards the Strait of Tiran, Israel's maritime gateway to Africa and Asia. The Egyptians have successfully blockaded the strait in the past, cutting off all shipping to and from Israel's southern port of Elath. Unless some formula for internationalizing Sharm-el-Sheikh can be found, the Israelis will probably insist on retaining control; they flatly refuse to hand it back to Egypt.

☐ *Gaza.* This strip of desert 25 miles long and 5-to-7 miles wide is populated by some 420,000 Palestinians, more than 80 percent of them refugees. It was originally intended, under the UN's 1947 partition plan, to be part of Arab Palestine. After the 1948-1949 Arab-Israeli war it was administered by Egypt; after the 1967 war, by Israel. The latter government has never formally expressed a desire for permanent control of the Gaza Strip. But as yet there is no consensus on whether it should eventually be ruled by Egypt, Jordan or a new Palestinian regime.

☐ *West Bank of the Jordan River.* This fertile agricultural region, which was to have been the heart of Arab Palestine under the UN's partition plan, was annexed by Jordan in the 1948-1949 war and then occupied by Israel in 1967. An Arab summit meeting in Rabat [Morocco] in late 1974 voted to give the PLO sole authority over any part of the West Bank (or Gaza) surrendered by Israel. (Some 650,000 Palestinians live there. . . .) King Hussein thereupon renounced his claim to the area: "The West Bank is no longer Jordan, and we have no place in the negotiations over its future." Up to this point the Israeli government had been prepared to negotiate the eventual return of the West Bank to Jordanian control, with certain geographical modifications and security precautions. But it is not yet prepared, as we have seen, to negotiate with the PLO for the establishment of an independent Palestinian state, on the grounds that such a regime would seek to swallow Israel.

☐ *Golan Heights.* For nearly twenty years, until Israel seized the heights from Syria in the 1967 war, Syrian artillery dominated and periodically bombarded some of Israel's most fertile northern valleys. The Israelis are determined not to let that happen again. The twenty or so new civilian settlements they have introduced into the Golan area "were not established in order to be evacuated," according to . . . [Prime Minister] Rabin. His government is prepared to negotiate no more than "cosmetic" changes—a few hundred yards here and there—in the present cease-fire lines under an interim agreement. But the Syrian government demands total Israeli evacuation of the heights. Some Damascus suburbs are almost within the range of Israeli artillery. Observers see little hope of breaking the deadlock unless Golan can be effectively neutralized under UN auspices.

☐ *Jerusalem.* This may be the toughest bone of contention of all. The importance of Jerusalem is not strategic but religious; the issue is less political than emotional. In 1967 the Israelis annexed the Jordanian eastern sector, which includes the ancient city and the various holy places venerated by Jews, Christians and Moslems. Reunited Jerusalem promptly became the capital of Israel. The Israelis are categorical: their sovereignty over united Jerusalem is nonnegotiable. But they guarantee that its holy places will remain accessible to visitors of all faiths who come in peace, and they are prepared to negotiate agreements with authorities of the various religions on the status of the non-Jewish places of worship. Among these places is one of the most revered shrines of Islam: the Dome of the Rock in old Jerusalem, from which spot the prophet Mohammed is believed to have risen to heaven for divine inspiration in his teachings. To the Arabs, perpetual control of this sacred spot by a Jewish authority is insupportable. Either east Jerusalem should be detached and restored to the control of a Moslem authority, they demand, or the entire city should be placed under international administration.

Eugene V. Rostow, a former under secretary of state, who . . . teaches at Yale Law School, urges that the goal of our policy for the Arab-Israeli problem be nothing short of peace—"a fair peace, a balanced peace, but peace, nonetheless, and not a truce, an armistice or a *modus vivendi.*"

Nothing better than an armistice has been attainable over the past quarter of a century. Can a definitive peace be achieved by the current diplomatic approach? Or would a different route be preferable in order to reach that elusive goal?

A Piecemeal Peace?

The Kissinger diplomacy that produced the two interim Sinai agreements is usually called the step-by-step approach. It has been criticized, as noted earlier, for sidestepping the core issues of the Middle East conflict. By concentrating on a few limited problems that are relatively easy to solve, it merely postpones the tough decisions and the moment of Arab-Israeli deadlock. Furthermore, say critics, the Mideast adversaries are encouraged to rely on secret deals through an outside mediator instead of negotiating openly and face-to-face—an essential requisite for any genuine, lasting settlement. Worst of all, perhaps, the euphoria generated by the Sinai "success" raises false hopes that the peace momentum can be sustained. Unfortunately there is no feasible next step. Israeli Defense Minister Shimon Peres announced . . . [in September 1975] that negotiations between Israel and Syria were many months away at best and that a resolution of the Palestinian issue was "a matter of years and years."

In defense of the piecemeal approach to peace, the following points are stressed: A sweeping, definitive Arab-Israeli settlement would, of course, be preferable to advancing one small step at a time. But until all the parties are ready to tackle the tough central issues in general negotiations—and so far they are not—we must welcome any progress that is possible. Each modest forward step reduces the danger of a new Mideast war, improves the political climate and buys some time to seek out a new era of agreement.

A Return to Geneva?

As an alternative to step-by-step diplomacy, it is often proposed that the international peace conference on the Middle East be reconvened. This gathering of foreign ministers was held in Geneva in December 1973, after the cease-fire of the October war went into effect. Egypt, Israel, Jordan, the United States and the Soviet Union took part in the conference, the two superpowers as cochairmen. UN Secretary General Kurt Waldheim attended as an observer. The Syrians were invited but declined to go; the Palestinians were never asked. The conference adjourned after two days with an announcement that it would reconvene "as needed in light of developments." Up to now [in early 1976] it never has (although the Military Working Group it created has met on several occasions).

Those who favor an early "return to Geneva" do not mean that this specific gathering must necessarily be duplicated. What they do urge is that Arabs and Israelis sit down together for *direct*, face-to-face negotiations with the aim of concluding a *comprehensive* peace treaty. These negotiations could be held anywhere, with as many interested outside powers attending as the participants wished. It is argued that the sooner the Arabs *un*affected by the Sinai accords are convoked to the peace table the better, since the risk of another war mounts every day that their aspirations are left unfulfilled. The Russians, too, should be reincluded in the peace-making process as soon as possible. They have been summarily by-passed by Kissinger's shuttle diplomacy, but their approval will be needed on any overall peace settlement.

Others, including the Ford Administration, are in no great hurry to see a return to Geneva. They grant that a conference of this sort will ultimately be needed to work out the final details of and ratify a general Arab-Israeli settlement. But for now, the immediate parties to the conflict seem more interested in the discreet step-by-step procedure. If they are pressured into a more public negotiating forum before they are ready, the result will only be a futile propaganda exercise. There are, moreover, some thorny problems to be smoothed out before a "return to Geneva." For example, should the Palestinians be represented at the next full conference? If so, by whom?

A Superpower Solution?

A corollary argument turns on the role of the United States and the USSR. Should the superpowers devise their own solution to the Arab-Israeli dispute and then jointly impose it on the parties with guarantees? Some feel this is the only practicable way of defusing the Mideast conflict and the risk of direct superpower confrontation there. The Mideast antagonists, they contend, have repeatedly failed to find a way of stabilizing the situation by themselves and would no doubt be relieved if a settlement were forced on them by the great powers. But others feel that no genuine, enduring peace can be imposed by outsiders.

The question of guarantees remains, regardless of which route is taken to the peace table. Once a settlement is signed, how can we ensure that its terms are strictly adhered to and both sides are protected from violations? (Although the Arabs far outnumber the Israelis, they claim to have as great a need of guarantees, on the grounds that Israel fired the first shots in two of the four wars—1956 and 1967.) Among the suggestions: Frontiers and demilitarized zones should be permanently patrolled by an international peacekeeping force under UN or other auspices. The force should include both Soviet and American troop contingents. It should emphatically *ex*clude them. American forces alone should be stationed on Israeli territory under a bilateral security treaty to guarantee the inviolability of Israel's permanent borders. A blanket embargo should be levied on arms shipments to the Middle East. And so on.

What more analysts agree on is the urgency of negotiations. Except for a limited respite purchased by last year's Sinai accord, maintains [former] Ambassador Yost, "time does not work in favor of Israel or peace. The double asset of oil and population means that the Arabs will almost certainly grow economically, militarily, technologically and internationally stronger over the next few years." The Arabs, adds Yost, will not tolerate the loss of their occupied lands indefinitely. So unless there is real progress toward a settlement . . . [before 1978 or 1979], he sees the chance of another Mideast war—more destructive than ever to civilian populations *and* more likely to involve the superpowers, unless they abandon their Mideast friends.

THE PLO: COMING ON STRONG [2]

The air raid sirens gave no warning. Screaming in over the Lebanese coast [in early December 1975], thirty Israeli jets caught the Palestinian refugee camps and neighboring villages unaware, strafing men and women at work and children at play. Ali Humani, thirteen, and Yusef Dib, eleven, were killed as they hunted birds with slingshots near the village of Bayyada in southern Lebanon. Nearby, another Israeli bomb killed a young mother as she nursed her seventeen-day-old baby. In all, at least 109 people were killed, according to the Lebanese body count, and two thirds of them were women and children. Israel announced that the Lebanese raids, the biggest in its history, were aimed at

[2] Article by Milton R. Benjamin, with Bruce van Voorst and Jay Axelbank, correspondents. *Newsweek.* 86:55-6+. D. 15, '75. Copyright 1975 by Newsweek, Inc. All rights reserved. Reprinted by permission.

breaking up concentrations of Palestinian commandos in the refugee camps. Politically, however, the attacks were a disaster for Israel. They set off a storm of international protest and handed the Palestine Liberation Organization another big boost.

The attacks were angrily condemned by Pope Paul and by many Western nations and produced another upheaval in the United Nations. Just two days before, the Security Council had decided to invite the PLO to address it for the first time at a debate on the Middle East in January [1976]. But when a special Security Council meeting was hastily convened late last week [in early December 1975] to discuss the attacks on Lebanon, the PLO was granted a place at the horseshoe-shaped table a month ahead of schedule. It was also accorded virtually the same status as a member nation—an honor never before granted a national liberation movement.

Boycott

The admission of the PLO to the debate produced an Israeli boycott of the session, which left the embattled Israelis more isolated than ever. While the PLO was riding high, Israeli Prime Minister Yitzhak Rabin issued his toughest statements since taking office in mid-1974. In an interview with *Newsweek* [magazine], he vowed that Israel would never negotiate with the PLO and warned that a new Mideast war might be closer than most people thought.

The initial PLO victory in the Security Council was the result of an eleventh-hour Syrian threat not to renew the mandate of the UN truce force on the Golan Heights. Syria insisted that it would allow UN troops to stay in the buffer zone for another six months only if the renewal resolution called for a new Security Council debate on the whole Mideast problem—with full PLO participation. Israel brought strong pressure on the United States to veto any such resolution, but the Ford Administration finally decided to support a compromise. The resolution itself did not mention the

PLO; it called only for a Security Council debate next January 12 [1976] on "the Middle East problem, including the Palestinian question." Soviet Ambassador Yakov A. Malik, the acting council president, then declared that the majority of the Security Council took this to mean that "representatives of the Palestine Liberation Organization will be invited to participate in the debate."

Bitter

The PLO triumph—and the US failure to prevent it—left the Israelis embittered and divided. Top government officials privately accused Washington of reneging on its promise to avoid dealings with the PLO until the commandos accept Israel's right to exist as an independent state. The Israeli government also seemed at a loss over what to do next. During a bitter six-hour cabinet debate, doves urged a new Israeli initiative on the Palestinian question, while hawks demanded expulsion of all UN forces from Israeli-held territory. The government finally voted to boycott the January debate and, as a further sign of defiance, to construct four more Jewish settlements in the Golan Heights.

The air strikes the next day against suspected PLO bases near Tripoli in the north of Lebanon and Nabatiye in the south upset many Israelis. Defense Minister Shimon Peres said the raids were prompted by solid intelligence reports that the Palestinian guerrillas were organizing new attacks on Israel. But Major General Aharon Yariv, a former chief of Israeli military intelligence, called the operation "self-defeating." "I would have to say it was a mistake," he complained in Washington. The leading Israeli newspaper, *Haaretz*, charged that the raids "merely fueled the present anti-Israel campaign in the world."

Emboldened by the outcry against the raids, Lebanon and Egypt demanded an immediate meeting of the UN Security Council, with Egypt pressing for PLO participation. A majority of the council quickly agreed to invite the PLO under Rule 39, which lets the Security Council hear parties "whom it considers competent for the purpose to supply it with information." But the PLO, which has had permanent observer status in the General Assembly since last year [1974], refused to join in under those conditions. It wanted to take part under Rule 37, which lets the council invite "any member of the United Nations" when its interests are affected. Even some backers of the PLO hesitated at that, but eventually the Palestinians prevailed.

The decision to tailor the rules to suit the Palestinians outraged the United States and Israel. [Former] US Ambassador Daniel Patrick Moynihan denounced the PLO as "an amorphous terrorist organization." Israel's envoy, Chaim Herzog, warned: "Tomorrow you'll have the Irish Republican Army sitting here."

Despite that unanimity, the relationship between Washington and Jerusalem was badly frayed. Diplomatic analysts continued to speculate about a statement delivered to Congress a month ago [in November 1975] by Deputy Assistant Secretary of State Harold Saunders. "The issue is not whether Palestinian interests should be expressed in a final statement, but how," Saunders declared. "There will be no peace unless an answer is found." In response to howls from Israel, Henry Kissinger dismissed the statement as an "academic exercise." But *Newsweek* learned that the Secretary of State had cleared the document in advance, and that it was intended, as one US official put it, as "an effort to unfreeze the Palestine debate."

For the moment, however, the Palestinians were not disposed to make any deals. Basel Amin Aql, the thirty-five-year-old native of Jaffa [Israel] who represented the PLO in the Security Council last week [in early December 1975], told *Newsweek* he still considered fighting more important than diplomacy. "The more we intensify our armed struggle, the more support we will get," he said.

The PLO's improving fortunes apparently prompted Egypt to mend its fences with the other Arabs three months after Cairo alienated many of them by concluding its Sinai disengagement agreement with Israel. Egypt's support for a strong PLO role in the Security Council seemed to be significant. And even as Egypt was reclaiming the Abu Rudeis oil fields, the main prize of the disengagement pact, it denounced Israel's raid on Lebanon as a "violation of the spirit" of that accord. Some diplomatic observers expected Egyptian President Anwar Sadat to adopt an even more militant stance once all the provisions of the agreement have been fulfilled next February [1976].

Already the Arabs and their allies in the UN were scoring points. They rammed a resolution through the General Assembly last week [in early December 1975] calling on member nations to halt military and economic aid to Israel. In the Security Council, five third world nations introduced a draft resolution condemning Israel's air raid and warning that any repetition might compel the council to take "appropriate steps." The United States hinted that it would veto such a measure unless all acts of violence in the Mideast were covered. But Moynihan carefully specified that Washington would "nether condone nor excuse" Israel's attack on Lebanon.

Warnings

Despite its growing isolation, Israel was determined to hang tough. Little time was lost in launching the four new settlements on the Golan Heights. By the weekend, workers were erecting barbed-wire fences around the chosen sites and trucks were bringing in prefabricated houses. The Rabin government also chose, for the first time, not to interfere with a group of right-wing Jews who pitched camp in Sabastiya in the occupied West Bank [of the Jordan River]. Instead of arresting the squatters, as they had in the past, Israeli soldiers lined up outside their field kitchen for hot coffee.

In both Israel and the United States, however, there were increased warnings that Rabin's government eventually would have to find some way of negotiating with the Palestinians. "Israel can't keep on saying 'no,'" declared the Israeli newspaper *Davar*. "We have to make some political preemptive strike." In Washington, Senator George McGovern stated flatly: "I don't think the Israelis can sustain their position of not dealing with the PLO." Some modest hopes were expressed for progress at the Security Council debate in January, and *Newsweek* learned that PLO leader Yasir Arafat currently had no plans to attend himself—which could help to reduce the tension. "We're essentially stymied at the moment," said a top US official. "Some 'give' by both sides in that debate could grease the slides." So far, however, the PLO's position was so strong—and Israel's so weak—that neither side seemed likely to concede very much.

SINAI PACT STIRS MISGIVINGS AMONG ARABS [3]

Many Arab diplomats, scholars and journalists outside Egypt, believing that the Sinai agreement has crucially weakened the Arab side, are convinced that the pact will prove an obstacle to peace rather than a step toward it.

Despite disclaimers by Anwar Sadat, the Egyptian president, these critics—Syrians, Palestinians and Lebanese—contend that Egypt, the most populous and militarily powerful Arab country, has been broken out of the Arab front against Israel.

They assert that, with American encouragement a psychological and political demobilization will take place in Egypt, with the result that the average Egyptian will become inward-looking and no longer concerned with the fate of the Palestinians, which is at the heart of the Arab conflict with Israel. It will take another war to reverse this trend, the critics of the Sinai agreement say.

The critics in Damascus and Beirut also charge that neither American nor Israeli attitudes have changed as a result of the agreement. They insist that the publication of the secret American-Israeli understanding revealed that the United States remained totally committed to Israel, to the

[3] From article by Henry Tanner, correspondent. New York *Times*. p 3. O. 11, '75. © 1975 by The New York Times Company. Reprinted by permission.

point of having given Israel veto power over any contacts between Washington and the Palestinians.

Advanced Arms an Issue

The critics note that Secretary of State [Henry] Kissinger has promised Israel $2 billion to $3 billion worth of advanced weapons, and they contend that it will be a long time —especially in view of the . . . [1976] American elections— before Mr. Kissinger or another Secretary of State, will even think of interrupting the new flow of weapons as a means of persuading Israel to make further withdrawals from occupied Arab territory.

This goes to the heart of the problem, as Arab scholars, journalists and politicians see it. These men are convinced that Israel will give up further ground in the occupied Syrian territory and the West Bank of the Jordan River only under sharp pressure from Washington.

Mr. Kissinger's reassurances to the contrary, they just do not see any such pressure before or soon after the American elections . . . [in 1976]. And this, in their view, means another stalemate and therefore drift toward another war.

A Palestinian university teacher said:

"You are doing what you always did. You say that you are making Israel strong because only strong Israel can make concessions. But the opposite is true. How are you going to prod them now? You have made them immune to your pressure for the next ten years."

For President Sadat the most important reason for wanting the Sinai agreement was that he thought—and still thinks—that it will lead to direct American involvement in the Middle East, on the Arab side as well as the Israeli.

The Egyptian leader had come to the conclusion that the Arab-Israeli conflict could not be solved and that Israel could not be induced to evacuate the territories she occupied in 1967 as long as one of the two superpowers—the United States—remained committed to the exclusive support of Israel while the other—the Soviet Union—gave more half-hearted backing to the Arabs.

It is also hoped that the mood resulting from the agreement will bring investors and industrialists from the West and the Arab countries into Egypt to help salvage her ailing economy.

Mr. Sadat's critics concede that their contention is based on the expectation that Mr. Kissinger will be unable to bring about another disengagement on the Syrian front.

Syrian, Palestinian and Lebanese critics fear that the agreement has isolated Egypt, neutralized President Sadat and muted the most effective moderate voice in the Arab world for the time being.

Assad's Role Weakened

Egypt, this reasoning goes, could be an effective leader toward a peace settlement only if she maintained her credentials as a confrontation state, along with Syria, and if she remained in a position to influence policies within the Palestinian liberation movement.

The critics further say that the Sinai agreement has weakened the position of President Hafez Assad of Syria in face of more unyielding officials in Damascus. This, in turn, has reduced his ability to enter into a disengagement agreement of his own, the critics add.

Specialists on Palestinian affairs moreover report that the Sinai agreement has strengthened the extremist leaders within the Palestine liberation movement and undermined the authority of such relative moderates as Yasir Arafat, who until recently had been working closely, if discreetly, with President Sadat.

Gain for Palestine Extremists

If the power struggle within Palestinian leadership culminated now, those who reject negotiation might well win, specialists here say. This was not the case a few months ago.

Negotiations are reported to be under way between Mr. Arafat and such extremist leaders as [Dr.] George Habash. The extremists are understood to be demanding that Mr.

Arafat denounce the Sinai agreement as "Egyptian treason" and that he publicly pledge not to attend any kind of Geneva conference no matter what the circumstances.

Arab critics of the agreement contend that American motives have once more become suspect among Arab nationalists. Extremists accuse Mr. Kissinger of deliberately seeking to split Egypt from the rest of the Arab world. Moderates say that whatever his intentions, this is the result by which the American action has to be judged.

A Syrian diplomat recalled that Mr. Kissinger, on his last visit after the agreement had been signed, told President Assad that the United States would try to "get something" for Syria before the American election but that "he could not promise."

"What kind of step-by-step is that?" the diplomat asked.

West European diplomats in the area moreover express fear that the United States will not be able to meet the hopes of economic assistance and investment in Egypt that have been created by the agreement.

The needs of Egypt are astronomical. And if President Sadat fails to solve his economic problem because the Arab oil producers are not willing to give the money that the United States cannot provide, then the agreement would lose its justification even in the eyes of many Egyptians, these diplomats say.

They point out that the only Arab leader who has publicly endorsed the Sinai agreement so far is President Jaafar an-Numeiry of the Sudan. King Khalid of Saudi Arabia was quoted by Mr. Kissinger as being in favor but has not said so himself, and others have been cautiously silent.

Alternative Suggested

A better approach to peace than the Sinai agreement, almost all critics say, would have been for the United States to start pushing for a final settlement, including Israeli withdrawal to the pre-1967 lines, in return for a real peace accord.

Informed diplomats . . . report that this actually was the approach chosen by Arabists in the US government earlier this summer, but that it was dropped as politically unfeasible because of expected opposition from Israel's supporters in Congress.

Criticism of the agreement is admittedly based on the assumption that Mr. Kissinger will not be able to bring about another disengagement on the Syrian front. If he did—and the chances seem slim—the first obstacle would be surmounted and momentum toward peace would be achieved, even his critics concede.

A CONVERSATION OVERHEARD [4]

In 1970, Ahmed, who was then a history teacher at a West Bank secondary school, decided to visit West Jerusalem, a mile and a half away, for the first time in his life. He had been thinking about it for three years, since the Israeli occupation in 1967. Late one afternoon, he entered West Jerusalem, walked past the Terra Saneta School, and down the street to a cafe.

The Cafe Savion looked more Arab than Israeli. It did not look European in any way, perhaps because of its wrought-iron doors. Ahmed entered the cafe, hesitated, and then walked over to a corner table. He was surprised when the waiter offered him Turkish coffee. As he sipped his coffee, he became aware of an Israeli sitting alone at the next table. The Israeli, a young man about Ahmed's age, smiled timidly at him.

Shlomo, the Israeli, had seen Ahmed enter the cafe and knew immediately that he was a Palestinian. He could also see Ahmed's uneasiness and hesitancy. Shlomo was lonely. His family lived in Tel Aviv. He thought that it was about time he talked with a Palestinian. He had a lot to learn about them. Besides, he had just graduated from the School

[4] From *The Middle East & the New Realism,* by Indar Jit Rikhye and John Volkmar. International Peace Academy. 777 United Nations Plaza. New York 10017. '75. p 55-60. Reprinted by permission.

of Sociology at the University of Tel Aviv and was starting his first job, at the Ministry of Health, the next day. He was excited about his new job. He wanted to tell someone about it.

He took a chance. When he saw Ahmed's expression after taking his first sip of coffee, he smiled.

"Not bad for Israeli coffee, is it?"

That broke the ice. Shlomo and Ahmed talked for an hour. But Shlomo felt that they had much more to say to each other. In their first talk, they had carefully avoided some issues on their minds which could not be discussed until they knew each other better. Shlomo proposed that they meet in a week, at the same time and place, for coffee. Ahmed agreed. They have been meeting ever since, even during the October war [of 1973].

It is November 23, 1974, Shlomo, now a department head at the Ministry of Health, sits at the corner table at the Cafe Savion. Ahmed, now the headmaster of the school, walks in and joins him. Shlomo's smile of welcome disappears when he sees the frown and concern on Ahmed's face.

Shlomo: Welcome, Ahmed. What will you have? The usual? . . . Waiter, bring a Turkish coffee, without sugar.

Ahmed: Things are very bad these days. It's as if the events of the past week have separated us even more and that hope for a lasting peace is dimmer than ever.

Shlomo: The . . . speech [of PLO leader Yasir Arafat] at the UN has shaken Israelis. Their attitudes have suddenly shifted to a much harder line. Every Israeli who could get to a television set watched the speech. Thy saw the gun at his hip, and when he ended by appealing for the right to establish a national independent state on Israeli land . . . well, that was too much. Even the moderates here are angry and are keeping quiet.

Ahmed: You Israelis have lost your senses over the speech. You refuse to recognize some things. Arafat is trying to keep the PLO elements satisfied. It's obvious to everyone that his demand for a secular democratic state for all of Palestine is to satisfy the more extreme groups in the PLO. It's a sort of "first price." When you buy a lamb at the market, you ask the first price without ever intending to pay it, don't you?

Shlomo: Arabs have not understood what Israel means to Israelis and to the Jews . . . [in other lands]. Why do you think that the most settled and successful Jew [living outside Israel] gives all he can to Israel and works for its survival? Because he feels that the survival of Israel is directly related to his own survival, to the survival of his family. Say he lives in Chicago. It's as if he had built a family-sized bomb shelter in his garden and had stocked it with food and supplies. He knows that the chances of a bomb falling on his garden are very slight, but in the back of his mind is always the nagging fear of another holocaust. He has an ever-present sense of insecurity. He wants to be ready for anything. All of a sudden you Palestinians come along and order him to take his shelter down, saying that you want to plant a tree in its place.

Ahmed: Those of us West Bank Palestinians who have lived under Israeli occupation since 1967 have lost their desire for a secular state where Jews and Arabs can live in peace. We're tired of living together. We long for our own state. Nothing personal, Shlomo, but you Israelis will never accept the Arab as an equal. Or anyone else, for that matter. You still believe that you are the "chosen people" and that Christians and Moslems and Buddhists are impure and inferior.

Shlomo: But Ahmed, look at Nazareth, where Jews and Arabs have lived together since 1948, and even before.

Ahmed: I went to Nazareth last year and saw how they live. Two separate towns, with the Jews in modern apartments high up on the mountain overlooking the old Arab quarter. How many Jews there talk to Arabs? That's not what is meant by a democratic secular state. No, we've got to make it clear to those PLO politicians in Beirut that we're not in favor of a secular state because it won't work. Maybe twenty-five or a hundred years from now, after we've lived as peaceful neighbors, we'll mutually agree that a confederation, or even a single state, is to our benefit. But not now. Not for some time.

Shlomo: But how do you get the message across?

Ahmed: Every summer, thousands of Palestinians visit the West Bank. They come to see relatives, but also to see Israel. Many of them do not remember their homes there; they were too young. Some go to Tel Aviv and Haifa for the first time. When they leave, they realize that the one thing that unifies Israelis and Jews all around the world is their determination to resist any move to dismember the state. Most won't admit it, but they are impressed with what they've seen. They begin to understand the futility of the extreme PLO position.

Shlomo: Yes, you're right about the unifying element. Even you would no longer be my friend if I thought you were working for the destruction of Israel.

Ahmed: At least allow us to think of the possibility of unifying someday. Allow us to dream, and understand that it is a dream and not a declaration of war.

Shlomo: Dream if you will, but don't make it a part of a peace agreement. You see, we Israelis believe that Arabs don't understand the true meaning of democracy. Israel is the only democratic country in the region. We practice democracy every day.

Ahmed: Damn it, look at all the Arabs and Palestinians who have settled in democratic societies in the United States and Europe. They assimilate quickly, conform to local laws and customs. Really, that is one of our problems. Once an Arab moves to a country like the United States or England he is almost totally lost to our cause.

Shlomo: You're right, of course. If the Arabs overseas ever began to resemble the Jews . . . [overseas], this problem would have been settled, one way or another, long ago. An Arab goes to the [United] States, for instance, gets his Ph.D., gets a post as a professor in some university there, marries an American girl, and that's it. He's lost to the cause.

Ahmed: Even worse, he comes to the Middle East for his summer holidays to visit his poor relatives, tries to tell us how to solve our problems, then returns to his comfortable life overseas.

Shlomo: So then you turn to [Jordan's King] Hussein to solve your problems for you. . . .

Ahmed: Anyway, we West Bank Palestinians don't want Hussein to deal for us. We've never trusted him. When we were under Jordanian rule, we suffered, too. I was a student then. We had organized pro-Nasser [the late Egyptian President Gamal Abdel Nasser] demonstrations in Nablus and Ramallah. Hussein sent his toughest Bedouin troops to the West Bank. Believe it or not, they machine-gunned the students.

Shlomo: So why do you complain so much about our occupation? We don't machine-gun your students.

Ahmed: Listen, Shlomo. I almost didn't come to meet you today. On my way here, I walked through the Old City and saw teen-age students being chased and beaten by your soldiers. Your soldiers are just kids themselves. The only difference is that they hold the guns. It makes me sick to stand by and do nothing. After seeing that, I really didn't know whether you and I could talk today.

Shlomo: I am truly very sorry about what is going on, Ahmed, as are other Israelis. There are some of us who are protesting to the government and asking how can we expect to live in peace with the Palestinians in the future if we are making bitter enemies of them today. We are overreacting to a few PLO flags waved in our faces by young students. The students don't know how we are feeling now about the PLO. It appears that we are trying to avenge Arafat's speech by taking it out on young students here. That's what some Israelis are saying.

Ahmed: You forget the past too easily. My father told me that when Israel was recognized as a state the Jews were in the streets demonstrating, shouting, and passing out wine to everyone. And then you turn around and condemn terrorism and call us animals. What about the murder of Count Bernadotte? What about the blowing up of the King David Hotel? Then there was the Deir Yassin and . . . [These and other acts of violence were committed by Jewish terrorist groups during the fight for the establishment of the state of Israel.—Ed.]

Shlomo: Let's not wallow in the past so much, if we want to . . .

Ahmed: You sound just like a government spokesman. Forget the past, you say. Let's look ahead. Listen, Shlomo, we are talking about the past because we are the ones who are living in the past. If we forget the past, then we give up all our claims. You want us to be quiet and to be satisfied with our refugee camps. You want us to live as third-class citizens in "all that land we Arabs own."

Shlomo: Ahmed, please, please calm down. We still believe in dialogue, don't we? You and I must continue to talk about these things even though we get emotional from time to time. I'll concede that Palestinians have rights and that they must be satisfied before we can live in peace in this region.

Ahmed: All right, Shlomo. How about another coffee? Then I've got to go. I have to attend a student meeting tonight. I'm trying to keep them calm, trying to urge them not to give the military governor of the occupied territories an excuse to close down the school. Education must be our priority for now. Those of us under occupation have few options.

Shlomo: I wish you luck. I know that you are working under very difficult conditions. Hold on for awhile. We are not the only ones, you and I, the only Arabs and Jews talking. Others are talking, too, and a good number of others wish they were.

Ahmed: We're not much closer to a solution, but I got some things off my chest that I have wanted to say for a long time. One of the reasons the students are so excited is that for the first time in more than twenty-five years we're being listened to. We're all getting things off our chests. So, I'll see you next week, right?

Shlomo: Right. Next week. And in the meantime, good luck, Ahmed.

V. THE ARABS AND THE SUPERPOWERS

EDITOR'S INTRODUCTION

Because of frequent wars, continuing political disputes, and the overriding importance of oil resources, the Arab countries occupy a central position in world politics. Rarely has a week elapsed in the 1970s without a major news story emanating from the Middle East. In recent years, the headline-making character of the Middle East has, if anything, intensified. It is an area in which superpower rivalries are focused, national interests clash, and explosive events occur one after another.

In their jockeying for positions of advantage, the United States and the Soviet Union have been at odds for decades in the Middle East. The stakes are tremendous. Not only is access to assured oil supplies at issue. Geographical, political, and strategic considerations also are important. The Soviet Union has tried, with some success, to woo the Arabs and establish military bases in the region, thus outflanking the North Atlantic Treaty Organization, the security alliance of the Western countries. Moscow has also attempted, again with some success, to establish itself in the Persian Gulf in order to exert influence in that critical oil area bordering the Indian Ocean.

The United States has countered these moves by trying to block the expansion of Soviet influence through economic and military aid programs and intensive diplomatic efforts. These policies have produced their share of positive results. Counted as US allies are Iran and Saudi Arabia and, of course, Israel. Egypt and Jordan are both friendly to the United States at this time. Syria and Iraq, conversely, lean toward the Soviet Union.

This section deals with Arab relations with the superpowers. The first selection is a speech by L. Dean Brown, president of the Middle East Institute, which examines the

Middle East in the framework of the events of the past decade as well as the realities of today. The second article discusses the American role. What are the stakes for the United States? What priorities must be weighed before any action can be taken? And what are the likely consequences of any actions taken today?

The final article is one by O. M. Smolansky, professor of international relations at Lehigh University. It concerns the role of the Soviet Union in the Middle East. Though a prime mover of events in the region for over twenty years (through its role as arms supplier for the Arabs), the Soviet Union today appears to some observers to have slipped a little in importance. With the United States playing a prominent role in Arab-Israeli negotiations and with Arab leaders displaying increasing nationalistic tendencies, the dream of Soviet domination of the Middle East seems to be fading.

NEW DIMENSIONS IN THE MIDDLE EAST [1]

Let's look at the Middle East. It is a strategic area.

a. Geography: It is a communications center including Suez.
b. Underground wealth: It has oil today; copper, phosphates, and other minerals are there.
c. It has a growing political/economic strength.
d. Trade and investment increase; it's a two-way street now.

The Middle East is the cradle of civilization where three great monotheistic religions had their start. It has also been torn by strife since time immemorial.

[The] United States has long had relations with the Arab world. Some of our earliest treaties were with Oman and

[1] From speech by L. Dean Brown, president, Middle East Institute, delivered at a symposium sponsored by Monex International, Ltd., Los Angeles, California, June 16, 1975. *Vital Speeches of the Day.* 41:647-50. Ag. 15, '75. Reprinted by permission. In March 1976 the State Department sent Mr. Brown to Beirut to offer his services as mediator in the Lebanese crisis.

Morocco. In late eighteenth century we paid tribute to Barbary pirates not to enslave our sailors. Now we select to pay another form of tribute every time we fill our gas tanks.

It was not until after World War II, however, that US interest grew to major proportions. Of primary importance was our support of the newly-born nation of Israel. Every President—every Congress—since 1948 has consistently, strongly reaffirmed this support. It is a keystone of America's Middle East policy.

Second has been the discovery of oil. Large investments were made by American companies. Oil from the Middle East became more and more necessary for the industrialized world.

We should also remember that we have long had an interest in the culture of the Middle East. American universities established in Beirut and Cairo have played a vital role in educating the youth of the Middle East and forming the professional classes in a score of countries.

The United States has a very special interest in the Middle East. This is maintaining political stability, or to put it more precisely, to support Israel's security and territory. This special interest is shared by almost no other country and confronts us with problems in the United Nations as well as in our relationships with other countries.

Events . . . [dating back to the mid-1960s] have given new dimensions to our thinking and our policies. This is how we see the Middle East. We believe:

a. [The] United States has vital political, economic, strategic interests.
b. [The] USSR believes it has the same or similar interests.
c. Possibility of confrontation exists.
d. US policy is continued support for Israel's security; yet, United States wishes to improve relations with the Arab world.

And the sharpness of the dilemma is posed anew each day

as we realize how dependent we will be on Middle East oil by the end of this decade.

Because of . . . [this dilemma the] United States has decided it must play a key role in the diplomatic negotiating process aimed at a peaceful and just settlement of the Arab-Israeli conflict. This role is accepted by Arabs. [Egyptian President Anwar] Sadat says only the United States has the power to affect change in the situation. [Israeli] Prime Minister [Yitzhak] Rabin . . . [says] the same.

In Middle East there are two other major US interests. First, . . . to prevent polarization and not let the region divide itself into a contest between extremes. To do so would invite outsiders to enter, perhaps to dominate. This is clearly *not* in the American interest. Second, . . . to help people to move forward on national development, recognizing fully that economic, political, and social progress comes only through a nation's own efforts; we can only help—never lead or direct.

As a whole, American interests are cohesive and sensible. They put a heavy strain on us.

Before we look further at the problems, let us examine some of the individual countries. Just as we cannot lump together all the countries of North and South America and distill . . . generalizations that apply equally to all, so we cannot lump together the Arab world.

It is disparate, different and divided. Throughout history Arab states have warred with each other, uniting only to conquer Spain, or menace France, or to drive the Crusaders out of Jerusalem, or—maybe now—to use the economic/financial power of oil to seize leadership of [the] third world and perhaps to confront the developed world.

Let us look first at Iran. It is not even an Arab country. It is Moslem in religion but Persian in thought, tradition and deed. It has been cool to [the] Arab cause; until . . . [the 1970s] it had close ties with Israel. Iran under the shah is confident. Sometimes it is aggressively confident. It is united, progressive and determined.

The shah wants a strong economy, translating today's oil wealth to tomorrow's industrial growth and agricultural modernization. Iran earned over $20 billion from oil in 1974. Despite enormous expenditures surpluses will rise in [the] next few years.

The United States and Iran . . . [in 1975] agreed that their mutual five-year goal should be $15 billion in nonoil trade. [The] United States will provide: $5 billion in general commodities, $5 billion in military equipment, and $5 billion in development goods.

Experts tell us that by 1980 expenditures can eat up surpluses derived from oil. The shah, however, seems determined to keep raising [the] price of oil as long as [the] costs of what he buys continue to rise. And I think no one should ever assume that the shah is only talking or can be persuaded by American bureaucrats that he should do otherwise than maximize his profits. Someone said he seems to act on whim; if so, he has a whim of iron.

It is perhaps strange to start with Iran in a talk about the Middle East. Historically, speakers on the Middle East talk of Egypt and Israel or perhaps Saudi Arabia. Historically, speakers have said that differences are so deep between Iranians and Arabs that they could never get together. These so-called truths are not valid . . . [in 1975].

Iran is an energetic galvanizer of change. Its military strength—its political drive—have made it a leader. With what results for [the] Middle East?

There are very important ones. Until . . . [March 1975] Iran and Iraq were antagonistic. The Kurdish problem . . . plagued their relationship. [Terrorist elements of the Kurdish minority in Iraq, who were militarily and financially supported by Iran, have been demanding, and occasionally fighting for, an autonomous province of their own.—Ed.] But . . . [in March 1975] the shah . . . abandoned support of the Kurds and their age-old dream of independence. Iraq and Iran signed an important agreement regulating problems including Iran's free access to the sea. There have been

—and will be—many changes flowing from this agreement. Obviously, each country can cut down the large military forces deployed on the borders. The consequences, if there is another Arab-Israeli conflict, are obvious. . . .

Saudi Arabia is another country in transition. The death of King Faisal [in 1975] will accentuate processes of change despite the smooth turnover of power to King Khalid. Tens of thousands of college graduates are coming on to scene, modernized, somewhat westernized; although we should not mistake American clothes or slang for attitudinal changes. These young people will want and will get—at least—evolutionary change. It could go further in the next decade.

Just as the United States has a Joint Economic Commission with Iran, so it has with Saudi Arabia. The two nations are embarked on an ambitious five-year plan. The fields covered are: manpower and education; science and technology; agriculture; and industrialization. . . .

The United States already sells $1 billion of goods a year to Saudi Arabia. New private projects are immense. One calls for the expenditure of $4.5 billion. It will use gas that has been flared up to now for industry, as well as electricity and water desalinization.

Iraq earned $6 billion from oil . . . [in 1974]. It too has an elaborate development program. . . . [In 1975] it is spending $4.5 billion, largely for farm machinery, trucks, and aircraft. . . . [In 1974] the United States sold $250 million of goods to Iraq. In 1972 sales were only $23 million.

Iran, Iraq and Saudi Arabia are three major oil producers. Kuwait, Oman and the United Arab Emirates cannot be forgotten. They have lots of oil and very few people. Kuwait's per capita income is [one of] the highest in the world. These states are the producers of cash surpluses. They simply can't spend their receipts as fast as our major suppliers. These . . . are Venezuela, Nigeria and Canada, and not Arab states as most believe.

The OPEC [Organization of Petroleum Exporting Countries] states accumulated $60 billion in surpluses in 1974.

Only about $11 billion was invested in [the] United States, most in government securities. The Treasury [Department] tells us that less than $1 billion went into stocks, corporate bonds, or real estate.

Sometimes we have [a] little trouble with OPEC. . . . They are not all Arab, by any means. OPEC started in 1960. It only became organized and strong in 1971, as we know from the gas lines of the winter of 1973-1974. OPEC countries have 66 percent of the world's oil reserves; the United States has 5 percent. The aims of OPEC are simple:

1. Get the price [of oil] up and keep it up.
2. Get ownership of wells; nationalize.

In 1938 the Middle East provided 7.7 percent of the world's [oil] production. In 1973 it was 49 percent. . . . [In 1975] it's about 55 percent.

The result of the price increase was dramatic. There was a huge flow of money to OPEC states. Huge debts—especially by poor countries—were incurred. . . .

Early estimates were that a trillion dollars would be accumulated by OPEC members by 1985. These estimates . . . [have been] scaled down considerably. Nevertheless transfers will be so great that financial institutions as we know them . . . will be different. One result already is that after West Germany, Saudi Arabia is second largest holder of gold, more than United States.

Why have I stressed these facts? Because they represent real change in the Middle East. Let us summarize what is new.

1. A self-confident politically aggressive Iran, firmly led by the shah.
2. A new ruler in Saudi Arabia.
3. An evolving Iraq, interested in development.
4. Enormous liquid wealth in Arab hands.

Other changes should be mentioned briefly. First, there is a more rational Syria under President [Hafez] Assad. In

September 1970 Syrian forces invaded Jordan. In mid-June 1975 Assad visited [King] Hussein to discuss Syrian-Jordanian cooperation.

Syria and Iraq remain at odds. Both are trying to settle contentious issues and move toward a unity in views on foreign policy issues.

Second, Jordan is stronger and more confident. Its economy, thanks to our help but also that of Saudi Arabia, Kuwait, Iran, . . . and the UN [United Nations] is booming. Its people are working. Jordan sees itself no longer as protector of the West Bank [of the Jordan River] and no longer as an outcast in the Arab world. Both views are highly significant as we examine [a] changing Middle East.

Third, Egypt under [President Anwar] Sadat is less politically aggressive and less polemic. It is pleased—almost deliriously so—to see the Suez Canal again operating. It is less prone to unilateral action and willing to take political gambles in step-by-step diplomacy. But it is also rearmed, stronger, more sure of itself, and confident of the future.

This leads to a fourth point. It is one not too well understood by Americans who have been convinced—one way or another—that the Arabs took a bitter beating in the October 1973 war. Arabs don't feel that way. They know they crossed the Suez Canal, which Western military experts had said was impossible. They fought well in [the] Golan [Heights]. They didn't run but inflicted heavy casualties.

And lots of Arabs took part, even if only symbolically: Moroccans, Saudis, Jordanians. A whole new psychology has been created in the Middle East. It is that Arab forces can stand up to Israel. . . .

Algeria has been a leader in confronting the West and the United States. It demands—not that oil producers help those who suffered most from price increases—but that developed nations share their wealth with [the] rest, that commodity and raw material prices be set and indexed to world prices, that a sort of automatic machinery be established to redistribute [the] wealth of the world, and that the marketplace—where prices are set according to supply and demand —be abolished.

Here is what forty nations said . . . [in March 1975] in Algiers. They called on the world for a "radical transformation in [the] structure of economic relations, which have been based . . . on inequality, domination and exploitation."

Some observers have gone so far as to say that [the] third world has declared war on the wealthier nations. Some say that the East-West conflict—which so long preoccupied Americans and the West, has become a North-South conflict. There is a lot of truth to these views. . . .

[In 1975] we face the possibility that the oil producers, who are among the wealthy, could opt for the mass of the poor.

Such an action could leave us exposed, almost alone, as other nations of the West either duck or hide. This is indeed a new dimension if, in addition to Arab demands for Jerusalem, for return to the 1967 frontiers, for a Palestinian state, is added a thrust toward a new economic order in which the United States pays for world peace by cutting its consumption, its production and in the end its military force. . . .

This can come about unless we act promptly. President Ford's reassessment of US policy becomes even more urgent. And let us hope assessment recognizes new dimensions of the Middle East.

Prolonged stalemate is no way out. If it doesn't lead to military conflict, it can lead to economic confrontation. . . .

[The] truth of the Middle East is more than the withdrawal from a few square miles of useless Sinai Desert. It requires solutions for: Jerusalem, West Bank, Golan, and Palestinian demands. What is at stake for Palestinians is the question of homeland. It is where people live; where they are born and where their parents are buried. The continued occupation of the West Bank where a Palestinian state could be, is one of the most basic, most intangible, most difficult problems to solve. . . .

This is the dilemma for the United States. Our commitment to Israel's security is solid and deep. American policy is to continue to supply weapons at constantly increasing cost to both United States and Israeli taxpayers, hoping that time is on our side or the problem will go away. It hasn't. It won't.

If [the] step-by-step [diplomacy of Secretary of State Henry Kissinger] fails, there are two recourses, according to President Ford. The first is the full Geneva conference. The second is Geneva, plus a return to step-by-step diplomacy.

There is another outcome: stalemate. This is the high-risk course. It could lead to the fifth battle in what is now [a] twenty-seven-year war, possible trouble with Soviets, to an oil embargo and real trouble for *all* the industrialized countries and probable disaster for the poor ones.

New decisions will have to be made by *all* the parties concerned as it could be fatal to stop the movement toward peace. Israel must decide what territory it will give up. Arabs must decide what concrete commitments they will make to peace. We—the West—and, no doubt, the USSR must decide how we can guarantee the results.

THE AMERICAN ROLE [2]

American weapons, American money and American political influence have played a role in the Mideast conflict for many years. . . . [In 1976] for the first time, American [observer] personnel are being committed to the front lines.

Sinai Commitment: Pro and Con

Our civilian observers in the Sinai mountain passes will not be defenseless. They will be allowed to carry pistols and rifles. UN troops will be patrolling their vicinity. And the President can immediately order them evacuated if he perceives a threat to their safety. Yet few dispute that, as one

[2] From "Arabs vs. Israelis." In *Great Decisions 1976*. Foreign Policy Association. '76. p 8-10. Reprinted by permission. Copyright, 1976 by Foreign Policy Association, Inc. 345 E. 46th St. New York 10017.

commentator wrote, the Americans "will be there, to some degree, as hostages. The operative principle, which has been applied to Berlin and Korea, holds that any nation, no matter how reckless, will think twice before it shoots at an outpost flying the American flag."

Although Congress gave its official approval to the Sinai commitment . . . [in fall 1975], the voices of disapproval have not been stilled. The loudest protest stems from fear that the United States may be slipping into "another Vietnam." Granted, say the protesters, that the Middle East in the mid-1970s differs in many respects from Vietnam in the early 1960s. Still, the pattern of creeping commitment—starting with a few hundred American advisers—could easily be duplicated. Our presence in Sinai is admittedly modest, even though it *is* costing American taxpayers at least $7 million to set up the facilities for the two hundred technicians and about $10 million a year to maintain them. But what kind of precedent will be established? How many more Americans will be needed in future to observe the peace along other Arab-Israeli fronts—the Golan Heights, the West Bank, the Gaza Strip, the entire Sinai peninsula? And what if another Arab-Israeli shooting war flares up in the Sinai? Will our personnel be caught in the crossfire before they can be evacuated?

Those who endorse the decision to send Americans to Sinai consider the risks to be "very modest" (Representative Morris K. Udall, Democrat, Arizona) and therefore acceptable. "I cannot say that they are immune from danger," acknowledged ex-Secretary of Defense James R. Schlesinger, but there are "substantial" safeguards. The Vietnam analogy is held to be false. There, we sent Americans to help one side fight a war; here, we are sending them to help both sides keep the peace. "I was present," recalls Speaker of the House Carl Albert (Democrat, Oklahoma), "when [then Secretary of State John Foster] Dulles told us that six hundred technicians would be sent into Vietnam and they would not be combat people. However," he adds, "I agree with . . .

[Secretary of State Henry] Kissinger's distinction here in the Mideast—it is not a going war, and we are not sending people in to help one side, but to observe both sides." To columnist Tom Wicker, the presence of Americans in Sinai makes another war there—a surprise attack from either the Egyptian or the Israeli side—less rather than more likely. And as for the financial expense, say the Administration's supporters, it is small indeed if compared to the cost of a fifth Middle East war—and the shock to the American economy from another Arab oil embargo.

Weighing Our Priorities

Oil, for our European and Japanese allies as well as for our own needs, is one of the most tangible interests we have in the Mideast region. Is it the most important? Here we come to the heart of the controversy over the American role in the Arab-Israeli dispute, namely: Just what are our policy priorities in that part of the world? . . .

[Professor Eugene V. Rostow, former under secretary of state,] believes that the problem requires "a national, and not a sentimental or a partisan approach. What is at stake for us in that feverish area should be examined in the perspective of the national interest, not of sympathy for either the Arabs or the Israelis. We can," he feels, "sympathize with both Arabs and Israelis, caught up in a web of history they did not make."

Fair enough, in theory. In practice, however, the debate is often colored by sympathy, sentiment, economic bias, cold war ideology or some other emotion that may distort perspective. For the purposes of this discussion, let us confine ourselves to the three main objectives that the Ford Administration is pursuing in the Middle East (listed here in no specific order of importance) and weigh the pros and cons.

Commitment to Israel's Security

In . . . [a June 1975 speech], Secretary Kissinger asserted that the United States would "protect *all* its interests" in the

Mideast. The word "all" was underlined in the text to stress that the United States had vital interests other than ensuring the survival of Israel. However, the commitment to Israel remains unwavering. No Administration has seriously considered loosening it since May 1948, when President Harry S Truman's was the first government to recognize the infant Jewish state.

Over its first twenty-five years of existence, Israel received a total of some $13.5 billion in economic support from abroad; about 80 percent of this came from private and official US sources. For the year 1974 alone, US military and economic aid reached a record $600 million. Ever since the [1967] Six-Day War the United States has been Israel's only foreign source of arms (up to June 1967, France had been its chief supplier). Some $985 million worth of US military equipment was delivered to Israel in 1974 (making it number 1 on the list of foreign customers) and an additional $2.1 billion worth was on order.

Yet Israel is not officially an American ally. There are no formal security ties of any kind between the two governments—not even the sort of executive agreement on base rights and aid . . . [set up for] the American military relationship with Spain or Thailand. Nor is Israel a significant economic partner. It has no particularly valuable commodity or technology to sell to the United States, and its purchases of US exports in 1974 amounted to $1.2 billion—on a par with Switzerland or South Africa. The American commitment to Israel rests on other foundations. There is the moral aspect, rooted in memories of the Jewish state's founding amid the ruins of the Nazi holocaust. "Israel is largely a creation of the conscience of the West, particularly that of the United States," former Senator [J. William] Fulbright has written. "For that reason alone, her survival qualifies as an American national interest." There is the cultural aspect, grounded in the fact that Israel is the only Middle East society that fully shares our Western values of political democracy and Judeo-Christian traditions.

Not least, there is the ethnic aspect. The so-called Israel lobby here in the United States is made up of fourteen national Jewish organizations claiming to represent the great majority of American Jews. The spearhead of their efforts is the Washington-based American Israel Public Affairs Committee (AIPAC), registered as a domestic lobby with both the House and the Senate. It concentrates on obtaining favorable congressional votes on aid and defense matters affecting Israel. . . .

A number of congressmen are among those who feel that Washington is too deeply committed to Israel—in their opinion, an intransigent military power with expansionist ambitions. Representative David R. Obey (Democrat, Wisconsin) says the United States has a moral obligation to provide Israel with enough aid to assure its survival. "We do not, however," he adds, "have a commitment to underwrite and encourage an Israeli foreign policy—born, though it is, of understandable frustration, pressure and fear—that is essentially immoderate and unrealistic, that is not responsive to new conditions in the Arab world. . . ." Obey feels that Congress should pare Israel's $2.3 billion aid request for . . . [1976] "substantially." The amount should be sufficient to keep Israel's economy viable and maintain its existing military capability, he says; but it should not be large enough to encourage Israel's leaders to think they can afford to mark time in the search for a peace agreement.

On the opposite side of the fence are Americans who feel that the Administration's "evenhanded" Mideast policy is not deeply enough committed to Israel. In this view, it is only when the Israelis feel strong and secure in the knowledge that they have the full backing of the United States that they can afford to be flexible in their dealings with the Arabs. The Israelis, it is argued, are much less convinced than the Ford Administration that the Egyptians sincerely want peace—and they have much more to lose if their suspicions are justified. A constructive policy step, in this view, would be a full-fledged security treaty between the United

States and Israel similar to the one between the United States and Japan. This would oblige Washington to commit American forces to Israel's defense if there is ever a grave threat to its survival.

Improved Relations With Arabs

Whether Americans in general would approve of a formal defense alliance with Israel, and whether the Senate in particular would ratify it, are moot questions. But American public opinion . . . appears a good deal more favorably inclined toward Israel than toward its adversaries. "The Arabs," concedes one of their American friends, "largely due to the Palestinian guerrillas, have been their own worst enemies when it comes to winning support in the United States for their cause."

The cultivation of better relations with the Arab world is now a high Administration priority. At a dinner that Secretary Kissinger gave . . . [in fall 1975] for the representatives of nineteen Arab countries, he told them that the United States had no interest or purpose in dividing them, for "only a united Arab world can make a final peace." He assured them, further, that US involvement in the effort to achieve that peace was "irrevocable" and "irreversible."

The only Arab country of consequence *not* represented at the gathering was Iraq—the sole government which has yet to mend the diplomatic links it broke with the United States in June 1967. (Economic links have, however, been growing.) The other "radical" front-line state, Syria, is on more amicable terms with America . . . [in 1976] than in many years, despite its continuing reliance on Soviet military support. Conservative Jordan has long been a good friend and arms customer of the United States. The Persian Gulf oil monarchies have traditionally been on cordial terms with Washington, and a special relationship, military as well as economic, has existed for some time between the United States and Saudi Arabia.

The most dramatic improvement in Arab-American relations, however, has been with Egypt. [President Anwar] Sadat's official visit to the United States last October [1975] underscored the end of a twenty-year estrangement. (This began when Washington refused aid for building the Aswan High Dam in 1955, and Cairo then turned to Moscow.) The Egyptian president has established good personal rapport with Secretary Kissinger and President [Gerald R.] Ford. But apart from that, he is convinced that the United States, and only the United States, is in a position to achieve a Mideast solution—precisely because of its special relationship with, and ability to exert influence on, Israel. The Administration, for its part, regards Sadat as a trustworthy and courageous statesman and considers a friendly government in Cairo to be pivotal to good American relations with the Arab world as a whole.

But there is one crucial element in the Arab equation with which the United States declines to have any official dealings at all: the Palestinians. The policy was reaffirmed at the time of the [September 1975] Sinai accord . . . , when Washington pledged that it would take no decision on dealing with the PLO until that group recognized the state of Israel and accepted the UN resolutions on principles of a peace settlement.

Washington does acknowledge that any genuine Mideast settlement "must take into account the legitimate interests of the Palestinians." But the prevailing attitude, similar to Jerusalem's, is that Jordan is the appropriate custodian of those interests.

The Israeli view of the PLO, which many Americans share, is that it is an outlaw gang of terrorists. But others dispute what they feel is an unfair "double standard" on Mideast violence. "Palestinian guerrillas have blasted civilians, booby-trapped buses, machine-gunned airport lounges and have killed indiscriminately," concedes senior correspondent Ray Vicker of the *Wall Street Journal*. "But the shattered bodies of women and children in southern Lebanese villages show that Israeli bombs and rockets can be just as deadly and erratic, too." Counter Israel's supporters: Israeli bombs and rockets are aimed at military targets and only in retaliation against Arab attack—not gratuitously or indiscriminately.

Senator Howard H. Baker, Jr. (Republican, Tennessee) was told by Crown Prince Fahd of Saudi Arabia that, in the latter's view, Yasir Arafat has the personal capacity to make the change from commando chief to responsible government leader. The transition, said Fahd, would be "almost automatic" if one condition were met: "that the United States recognize him."

But to many it would be unthinkable for the United States to bestow the accolade of official recognition on the Palestinian guerrillas. On the contrary, they argue, Washington has already gone too far—impelled by its fear of another oil cutoff—in its courtship of the Arabs. Senator Jacob K. Javits (Republican, New York) says he concurs with Kissinger that "*all* of the interests of the United States must be considered" in the search for a Mideast solution. But "some must be given precedence. In my judgment, one of the most important of our interests in that area is to preserve within secure borders a state that has been an unwilling participant in four wars . . . [whose people] ask for nothing more than respite from perpetual conflict."

The Soviet Factor

A somewhat different emphasis on US priorities in the Middle East is put forth by Professor Rostow. "The first and most basic," as he sees it, "is the geopolitical importance of the Middle East to the defense of Europe." For twenty years, he continues, the Soviet Union has pursued a strategy of enveloping NATO. It has exploited the Arab-Israeli confrontation and has poured massive amounts of economic, military and technical aid into the Arab world, making "considerable progress" from Iraq and Aden to Algeria. It is obvious that "hegemonial control of the oil, the space and the mass of the region by the Soviet Union would carry with it

dominion over Western Europe as well." Thus, concludes
Rostow, our political and strategic goal in the Arab-Israeli
conflict "should be to convince the Arabs that their flirta-
tion with Soviet policy can bring them nothing but tragedy,
and to insist on a fair and evenhanded peace . . ."

Others, including the Administration, believe that the
competition for influence is not the only significant aspect
of the Soviet-American relationship in the Middle East. At
least as important is the need to avoid direct confrontation
and to preserve the fragile superpower *détente*. Under Secretary of State Joseph J. Sisco feels that the United States and
the USSR have no basic conflict of interest over the Mideast,
as they do over strategic arms, trade, Berlin and some other
issues. Rather, he thinks they have a parallel interest in
stabilizing the region, since neither superpower stands to
gain from another war. . . .

[In 1976] the Russians find themselves somewhat out in
the diplomatic cold, having been upstaged by Kissinger's
performance on the Sinai pact. Their influence and prestige
in the Arab world are at the lowest ebb in years. They have
been virtually dismissed by Egypt and are getting cooler
treatment from both Syria and Iraq; their most intimate
Arab clients at the moment appear to be the Palestine commandos. They suffer from a further diplomatic handicap of
having no official communication channel to Israel. Diplomatic ties were severed in June 1967, although Moscow has
lately shown interest in restoring them. Foreign Minister
Andrei Gromyko has held several private meetings with
high Israeli officials. And at a Moscow dinner for the Syrian
foreign minister . . . [in spring 1975] he publicly offered the
Soviet Union's "strictest guarantees" under an "appropriate" peace agreement of Israel's security within its pre-1967
borders.

Professor Rostow himself acknowledges that it is "a fan-
tasy to suppose that the Soviet Union can be excluded from
the process of making peace in the Mideast." Thus he urges
that the only sensible goal for our diplomacy "is to induce

the Soviets to accept peace based on the Security Council resolutions for which they voted."

Which aspect of the Soviet-American relationship in the Middle East—competition for influence or collaboration toward a settlement—should figure most prominently in American policy for the region? How, if at all, can we hope to reconcile the two aspects? Or, as a third alternative, should we switch to a less active role altogether, on the grounds that there is no compelling need for us to compete with the Russians in the Mideast arena and that the Mideast antagonists are best left to work out their own solutions by themselves?

How deeply, in other words, do we want America to be involved in that part of the world? "I think," Under Secretary Sisco has said, "a final resolution of the Arab-Israeli dispute is doable—and only the United States can bring it about." Is he right or wrong?

THE SOVIET ROLE [3]

The Arab-Israeli war of October 1973 seems to have benefited the USSR in a number of different ways. Russian-trained-and-equipped Egyptian and Syrian forces performed unexpectedly well. As a result, Soviet influence in Cairo and Damascus is thought by many to have increased dramatically. The oil embargo, accompanied by a sharp rise in the price of petroleum, put severe political and economic strains on the Western alliance. Making use of widespread fuel shortages, the USSR sold oil to a number of West European countries, to Japan, and, according to some reports, to the United States as well, charging the fluctuating market price of $12 to $18 per barrel. Moreover, both before and after the war, Moscow sold large quantities of modern weapons to a number of Arab states. Unlike many earlier deals, payment was in hard currency.

[3] From "Soviet Policy in the Middle East," by O. M. Smolansky, professor of international relations, Lehigh University. *Current History.* 69:117-20+. O. '75. Reprinted by permission.

Outside the Arab-Israeli sector, the Soviets have also gained (albeit indirectly) from the . . . [1975] internal upheavals in Cyprus, Greece, and Portugal. Combined with the endemic political tensions in Italy, these instabilities have severely detracted from the cohesiveness of NATO's [North Atlantic Treaty Organization] "southern flank." Still, Soviet diplomatic options in these various situations are sharply limited; moreover, in almost every case each available course has inherent drawbacks. Thus, while obviously enjoying the predicament of Washington and its allies, the Kremlin has not been able to use their problems to any substantial advantage.

Nevertheless, what may be seen as a potentially lethal threat to NATO's solidarity, accompanied by what some perceive as a sharp increase in Soviet influence in the Persian Gulf and the Arabian Sea areas, have led many Western observers to conclude that Moscow's star has been steadily ascending in the Middle East since its nadir in July, 1972, when most Soviet military personnel were evicted from Egypt. However, a closer look at the situation calls such a conclusion into question.

In the eastern Mediterranean the USSR has maintained a basically passive position and may be said to have benefited indirectly from the difficulties experienced by the United States; in contrast, in the Persian Gulf, it has pursued an active policy but has not been able to prevent a decline in Soviet influence. The region's militarily strongest, economically most developed and populous state is Iran. . . . [Since the early 1970s] Shah Mohammed Reza Pahlevi has expanded economic cooperation with the USSR but relations between the two countries, while cordial, have not been close. If anything, they began to deteriorate again in the 1970s, when Teheran emerged as the leading opponent of "foreign interference" in the affairs of the gulf.

The events of the post-1973 period, above all Iran's newly found wealth resulting from the increase in the price of oil and her massive purchases of US military equipment, have made Iran the dominant regional power in the gulf, and have also prompted the shah to pursue an active policy of *rapprochement* with neighboring Arab states. His efforts have met with the approval of the conservative Arab governments, led by Saudi Arabia, as well as Egypt and . . . Iraq. The Kremlin, it may be assumed, has not been happy with this turn of events. The shah, who harbors the traditional Iranian mistrust of the "northern neighbor," has strengthened the determination of the conservative Arab rulers of the gulf to resist Soviet encroachments. He has also succeeded in driving a wedge between the USSR and Iraq, which, in the late 1960s and early 1970s, had emerged as one of Moscow's closest friends in the Middle East.

The tenuousness of the . . . Soviet position in the gulf is further illustrated by . . . events in Iraq. In the process of growing cooperation between the two countries, "sanctified" by the 1972 Treaty of Friendship, the Iraqi army was reorganized and equipped with modern Soviet weapons. The Russians also participated in the exploitation of the North Rumeila oil fields, in the development of a number of industrial projects, and in the building of a deep-sea port at Umm Qasr on the Persian Gulf, where Soviet naval vessels have since made frequent calls. In return, Iraq supplied the Soviet Union with oil. Moscow's hold over Baghdad, many analysts assumed, was substantial. However, as is frequently the case in Middle Eastern politics, appearances may have been misleading.

Signs of potential problems awaiting the Kremlin in Iraq have been in evidence for some time. The ruling socialist Baath party, from its inception, has been ideologically opposed to communism. Although it was overshadowed by larger and more important *raisons d'état*, this doctrinal antagonism precluded real intimacy in Moscow-Baghdad relations. In addition, various aspects of the Soviet petroleum policy, particularly during the post-October, 1974, embargo, contributed to Iraq's growing disenchantment with the USSR. (Iraq had earlier bartered some of her oil for

Soviet military and economic aid.) Not only did the Russians insist that Iraq fulfill her contractual obligations by supplying petroleum at pre-embargo prices, they did not join in the embargo (though encouraging the Arabs to persist in it) and actually increased their own exports to the consumer nations. Iraq's objection that her oil was resold in circumvention of the embargo and at an enormous profit (netting Moscow an estimated $3 billion) was countered by Soviet assurances that imports were being used only in the Soviet Union and East Europe. For obvious reasons, this situation created considerable resentment in Baghdad and elsewhere in the Arab world.

Iraqis were also unhappy with the quality of Soviet goods and services and with Moscow's frequent inability to adhere to agreed-upon timetables. Finally, the Kremlin made no secret of its displeasure with the Baath's determination to "settle" the Kurdish problem. A decisive defeat of the 2.3 million Kurds, who inhabit Iraq's oil-rich northern provinces, would deprive Moscow of important leverage on Baghdad. Once the Baath decided on an all-out war, the Soviets had no choice but to go along. But their initial attitude—including attempts to dissuade Iraq from an effort to crush the Kurds—must have been very disturbing to Baghdad.

As it turned out, the Kurdish war provided the Baath with the opportunity to reassert its independence from Moscow. As the Iraqis were pressing their fight against the rebels (who, because of the traditional hostility between Baghdad and Teheran, were being aided by Iran), it occurred to both governments that a resolution of the conflict could be of considerable mutual advantage. It would preclude the possibility of a major war between the two states. And in exchange for an opportunity to crush the Kurds, Iraq was prepared to settle her many differences with Iran. The agreement, concluded in Algiers on March 6, 1975, resolved most of the problems outstanding between the two gulf states and opened the door to unprecedented *rapprochement.*

The Soviet Union, reportedly surprised at the scope of the Iraqi-Iranian accommodation, may be expected to be the major loser politically. In one of the early manifestations of the new situation in the Persian Gulf, Saddam Husein, deputy chairman of Iraq's Revolutionary Command Council, publicly endorsed a gulf security pact, an idea long favored by the shah. In addition to mutual guarantees of the independence and territorial integrity of the signatories, the document is likely to demand the removal from the gulf of the military and naval presence of outside powers. In practice, this turn of events would result in the abandonment by the United States of its minor naval outpost on the island of Bahrein; but it would also mean the virtual exclusion of the USSR from the Persian Gulf, where the Soviets have been hard at work to establish and maintain a political and military presence. It would, moreover, leave the gulf under the control of mostly conservative, pro-West, and anti-Soviet regimes.

Additional evidence of the deteriorating Soviet position in Iraq is provided by Baghdad's economic activities. Since February, 1973, when the Baath resolved its longstanding dispute with the . . . Iraq Petroleum Company, the USSR and its satellites have not gained a single major contract in Iraq. Instead, Baghdad has greatly expanded its economic dealings with the West. (For example, US exports to Iraq have increased from $32 million in 1971 to $285 million in 1974.)

Nonetheless, the Soviet Union maintains a certain leverage in Baghdad, which continues to rely on Moscow for much of its military equipment and spare parts. But, as in the case of Egypt, this dependence has not conferred on the Russians the ability to control the actions of the Iraqi government. It remains to be noted that elsewhere in the gulf the Kremlin has not made much headway; most conservative regimes, led by Saudi Arabia, have tolerated only the most superficial dealings with the USSR.

Successful Policy

In the neighboring Arabian and Red seas area, the Soviets have scored some significant successes but have also suffered reverses. As a result of the abortive Communist coup in 1971 and the Saudi-inspired revolution of 1974, anti-Soviet regimes have come to power in Sudan and northern Yemen respectively. In contrast, in southern Yemen (the People's Democratic Republic of Yemen or PDRY) and the Somali Democratic Republic (Somalia) the USSR appears to have acquired relatively reliable clients. Both have professed adherence to "scientific socialism"; both have established close political, military, and economic ties with the Soviet Union; and both have placed some of their military and naval facilities at Moscow's disposal.

As impressive as these gains may seem at first sight, there are reasons to believe that even in these two states the Soviet position is not so secure as many assume. Generally speaking, as has been true elsewhere in the Arab world, deep involvement exposes the USSR to the vagaries of local and regional politics. At the moment [in late 1975], the internal situation is stable in Somalia, but the PDRY is experiencing political problems that may one day result in the ouster of the present pro-Soviet regime. Moreover, both governments, whatever their professed ideologies, are deeply nationalistic and acutely sensitive to the appearance, let alone the substance, of foreign control. They are not likely to tolerate Moscow's attempts to dictate their policy. (Indicative of this spirit is their determination to maintain cordial relations with Communist China.) Thus, even though their relative isolation from the mainstream of Arab politics has forced both states to seek Soviet backing, changed conditions may easily lead—as in the case of Egypt—to new foreign policy departures.

In short, while the USSR continues to enjoy a privileged status in Somalia and the PDRY, it would be premature to write them off as having moved into the Soviet orbit. Should a change in their political orientation occur, Moscow would suffer another major political setback with serious consequences for the strategic position of the Soviet Union in the Red and, especially, Arabian seas.

Soviet Setbacks

. . . [Since 1972] Soviet setbacks have been most visible and dramatic in the southern Mediterranean and the Arab-Israeli sector of the Middle East. Egypt is a case in point. The most populous, industrialized, and culturally advanced Arab state, it has been the object of keen Soviet interest since 1955, when Soviet Premier Nikita Khrushchev "discovered" in Egyptian President Gamal Abdel Nasser a "positive neutralist" leader, whose anti-Western stance merited Moscow's support. It is also worth recalling that it was Nasser who, in the aftermath of the 1967 [Six-Day War] defeat, made Egyptian naval and air facilities available to the USSR in exchange for protection against deep penetration raids by the Israeli air force. In July, 1972, in a major policy reversal, Nasser's successor, Anwar Sadat, deprived the Russians of the use of Egypt's air bases (some naval facilities remain at Soviet disposal) and ordered the evacuation of most of the Soviet military advisers.

The 1973 war, marked by Moscow's military and political support of the Arabs, did not result in any marked improvement in Soviet-Egyptian relations. Sadat and Syrian President Hafez Assad decided to go to war partly because of apprehension that, concerned with the larger issues of détente, the superpowers had informally acquiesced in the post-1967 status quo, which left Israel in control of Egyptian and Syrian territory. Persuaded of Moscow's and Washington's indifference and exposed to internal pressures, the two leaders decided to seize the initiative. They calculated, correctly, that a major crisis in the Arab-Israeli sector was bound to reawaken the Soviet-American competition, so necessary for wresting political concessions from Jerusalem.

What transpired subsequently has been most annoying

to Moscow. Sadat was aware that the United States alone is in a position to extract concessions from Israel—the Soviet Union simply does not have that kind of leverage in Jerusalem—and was not averse to snubbing the Russians. Thus he wholeheartedly embraced US Secretary of State Henry Kissinger's initiative, designed to seek phased Israeli withdrawal from the territories occupied in 1967. Vexed by Washington's unilateral approach to the solution of the Arab-Israeli conflict—a move designed to isolate the USSR and restore the United States to a position of political primacy in the Middle East—and equally upset by Sadat's willingness to accommodate Kissinger, the Kremlin argued that "step-by-step" diplomacy could at best produce "partial solutions." The Soviet Union went on to say that only the Geneva peace conference, presided over by the United States and the Soviet Union, would guarantee a "just and durable peace." In an attempt to apply additional pressure on Washington and Cairo, the USSR also officially endorsed the principle of Palestinian representation at Geneva and expressed itself in favor of the creation of a Palestinian state.

On a practical level, Moscow resumed large-scale arms shipments to Syria, where Assad, for reasons of his own, has doubted US willingness to force Israel out of the territories occupied in 1967. As a result, by 1975, the material losses suffered by Damascus in October 1973 had been replaced. The Soviets also agreed to a ten-year moratorium on the repayment of the Syrian debt. In Egypt, in contrast, the USSR not only refused to replace the war losses but actually withheld equipment promised under the terms of agreements concluded prior to October, 1973. Similarly, Moscow has refused to discuss with Cairo (whose economic plight has been rapidly reaching crisis proportions) the possibility of temporarily freezing Egyptian debt payments, on a debt variously estimated at $4 to $7 billion. Limited arms shipments were resumed in January, 1975, but, according to Sadat, the war losses have not yet been restored. As a result, relations with Egypt remained strained.

Partly in an attempt to counterbalance the deterioration of its position in Cairo, the USSR stepped up its efforts to improve relations with Syria and Libya. Suspicious of US and Israeli intentions, Assad's stand complemented the objectives of Soviet Middle Eastern diplomacy. For this reason, Moscow rewarded Assad with weapons and continued economic aid. (Over the years, the Russians have played an important role in expanding the country's economic infrastructure.) However, this extensive Soviet-Syrian cooperation must not be construed as indicative of subservience by Damascus to the Kremlin in matters considered vital by the Assad government. For instance, the latter has chosen to continue its feud with Iraq and, in so doing, has contributed to the failure of Moscow's efforts to create a united Arab front intended to deal with Jerusalem as well as Kissinger's attempts to resolve the Arab-Israeli impasse.

Assad has also cultivated cordial relations with conservative regimes, above all Saudi Arabia and Kuwait, whose large-scale financial assistance has made him more independent of the Soviet Union than the latter would prefer. Finally, Syria has consistently refused to sign a treaty of friendship with the USSR.

Libya is another Arab country . . . being courted by the Soviets. Relations between the two states have been poor both before and after the 1969 revolution that was headed by Colonel Muammar al-Qaddafi, a militant Moslem, whose religious zeal has precluded much cooperation with a Communist regime. Nevertheless, Moscow and Tripoli took the initial step toward cooperation in 1972, when they signed an agreement providing for limited Soviet economic and technical assistance in Libya. Another trade accord, as well as the first arms deal, were signed in May, 1974, followed, one year later, by a major arms agreement. (Under its terms, Libya will receive modern weapons valued at approximately $1 billion.) Concluded during Soviet Premier Aleksei Kosygin's May, 1975, visit to Tripoli, it was only part of a comprehensive aid program that also includes assurances of technical and cultural cooperation and Moscow's obligation to assist Libya with the construction of a nuclear reactor.

Sadat has insisted that the new accord provided for the establishment of Soviet naval and air bases in Libya, but these claims are as yet unsupported. (In the past, Tripoli has consistently refused to grant the USSR even limited port facilities. It remains to be seen whether this fundamental position will be changed as a result of the 1975 agreement.)

While it is highly doubtful that the new arrangement signals the "satellization" of Libya or that either the Kremlin or Qaddafi has had a change of heart, it appears in retrospect that the Middle East situation of the post-1973 period suggested a *rapprochement* from which both sides could hope to derive substantial short-range benefits. Tripoli, politically isolated from most of the Arab world and highly vulnerable to a possible Western attempt to seize Libya's oil fields in case of another Arab-Israeli war and the inevitable embargo, is attempting to bolster its position by accepting a limited Russian military presence. The Soviets, in addition to acquiring more hard currency, are trying to establish another operational base in the southern Mediterranean and to use Qaddafi as additional leverage on Sadat.

However, the long-range consequences of the Moscow-Tripoli *rapprochement* are not likely to live up to the Kremlin's apparent expectations. As long as Qaddafi remains in power, his anti-Communist attitude and his unpredictability are bound to create problems for the USSR. Even if he were removed, barring the advent to power of an openly pro-Soviet regime—an unlikely proposition—Libya's wealth and the strong Arab nationalist sentiments of her military may be counted on to preclude the establishment of Russian influence in that country.

In another attempt to reverse an unfavorable trend and to counteract the growing US influence in the Arab world, the USSR openly criticized US President Gerald Ford's Administration for its efforts to mediate the Arab-Israeli dispute. Soviet leaders urged that the negotiations to break the deadlock be transferred to Geneva where, as cochairman of the conference, the USSR would enjoy equal status with the United States. Once Kissinger's "shuttle diplomacy" was grounded in March, 1975, the Soviets stepped up their campaign for an early resumption of the Geneva conference. As far as the Kremlin was concerned, the basic prerequisite for success was the creation of a common Arab position with which to confront Israel and the United States. With this in mind, Iraq's strongman, [Vice President] Saddam Husein, the foreign ministers of Egypt and Syria, and [Al] Fatah leader Yasir Arafat of the Palestine Liberation Organization were invited to Moscow for exploratory talks. Simultaneously, negotiations were conducted with Israel, in Jerusalem, by two officials of the Soviet foreign ministry, and in Washington, where the Soviet and Israeli ambassadors held several meetings. In addition, the chairman of the Soviet delegation to the Geneva conference went to Amman to sound out Jordan's King Hussein. At that juncture—May and early June, 1975—Moscow's proposal for a settlement consisted of three basic propositions: (1) Israeli withdrawal from occupied territories; (2) firm guarantees of Israel's independence and territorial integrity; and (3) the establishment of a Palestinian state (presumably on the [Jordan River's] West Bank and in [the] Gaza [Strip]).

Not unexpectedly, the Kremlin ran into difficulties on all counts, with most of the parties concerned. Israel proved reluctant to part with much of the territory she had acquired in 1967. Promises of Soviet guarantees, while appealing to Jerusalem, were not sufficient to induce Israel to compromise what she considered the country's national security. Moreover, the manner and the timing of the Soviet proposal—made by Soviet Foreign Minister Andrei Gromyko at a dinner honoring the Syrian foreign minister—while dramatic in their impact—were not calculated to endear the USSR to the Arabs.

The Kremlin was equally unsuccessful in its efforts to create a united Arab front. Iraq and Libya have persevered in their refusal to discuss anything but an unconditional Israeli withdrawal from all occupied territories. Further problems arose when even those Palestinian groups that favor cooperation with the USSR were divided over whether to accept a truncated Palestinian state on the West Bank and Gaza in exchange for a recognition of Israel's right to exist as an independent state. Finally, some Arab leaders, including Sadat, showed marked reluctance to go to Geneva and preferred continued US mediation of the Arab-Israeli dispute. They felt that the Geneva conference would be useful only as a propaganda forum, but one whose likely failure would leave them no choice but to start another war.

Thus, having progressed from the position of a passive critic to that of an active participant and organizer, the Soviet Union soon discovered that, at this stage, little except meaningless propaganda "victories" could be expected from the Geneva meeting. In mid-June, the Soviet government announced that it had dropped its plans for an early reconvening of the conference. A decision on a new course of action was expected after the meeting between Kissinger and Gromyko, held in Geneva in July 10-11, 1975. However, . . . little progress was made. Thus, having seized the initiative in the wake of Kissinger's failure in March, Moscow had to abandon it in June. In the process, it tacitly admitted to another failure of Soviet diplomacy in the Middle East.

Conclusion

On balance, it would appear that while the USSR is not likely soon to lose its influence on the Arab world, Western fears of spectacular Soviet successes are often grossly exaggerated. In controlling arms deliveries to countries like Egypt, Syria, Iraq, the PDRY, Somalia, and, to a lesser extent, Libya and Algeria, the Kremlin has an ace in the hole that no Arab leader is likely to disregard; however, dependence in international politics is a two-way street. The donor can always back out of any given arrangement, but he can do so only at the risk of a severe strain in his relations with the recipient. In this instance, a cutoff of all military aid to any Arab state is bound to wipe out whatever advantages Moscow may have secured by means of previous programs.

In conclusion, an impartial observer must be amazed at the persistence with which the Soviet leaders have attempted to manipulate Arab politics in spite of the occasional danger (the increased threat of a war with the United States) and the frequent pitfalls inherent in such efforts and in spite of some painful lessons that the men in the Kremlin must have absorbed during their twenty-year-involvement in Arab affairs. It was probably unrealistic to expect the post-Stalin leadership to resist the temptation of active involvement in the Middle East—the rewards in the form of undermining Western positions and establishing Soviet influence were too alluring and the chances of gaining its objectives appeared reasonably good. But in 1975, even the most obtuse Soviet functionaries must face the fact that where others have failed they, too, are likely to fail. To "manage" the Middle East is a task beyond the ability of the outsiders, especially when they insist on working at cross-purposes.

BIBLIOGRAPHY

An asterisk (*) preceding a reference indicates that the article or a part of it has been reprinted in this book.

BOOKS, PAMPHLETS, AND DOCUMENTS

Burrell, R. M. The Persian Gulf. Library Press. '72.

* Christopher, J. B. Middle East—national growing pains. (Headline Series no 148) Foreign Policy Association. 345 E. 46th St. New York 10017. '61.

First, Ruth. Libya: the elusive revolution. Penguin. '74.

Foreign Policy Association. Great decisions 1973. The Association. 345 E. 46th St. New York 10017. '73.

Foreign Policy Association. Great decisions 1974. The Association. 345 E. 46th St. New York 10017. '74.

* Foreign Policy Association. Great decisions 1975. The Association. 345 E. 46th St. New York 10017. '75.
  Excerpts reprinted in this book: The oil states of the Persian Gulf. p 71-2+.

* Foreign Policy Association. Great decisions 1976. The Association. 345 E. 46th St. New York 10017. '76.
  Excerpts reprinted in this book: Arabs vs. Israelis. p 1-10.

* Gallagher, C. F. A note on the Arab world. (Southwest Asia Series. v 10, no 8) American Universities Field Staff, Inc. 535 Fifth Ave. New York 10017. '61.

Gervasi, F. H. Thunder over the Mediterranean. McKay. '75.

Halliday, Fred. Arabia without sultans: a political survey of instability in the Arab world. Vintage.' 75.

Hitti, P. K. Islam: a way of life. University of Minnesota Press. '70.

Hitti, P. K. A short history of the Near East. Van Nostrand. '66.

Hurewitz, J. C. The Persian Gulf: prospect for stability. (Headline Series no 220) Foreign Policy Association. 345 E. 46th St. New York 10017. '74.

Kerr, M. H. ed. The elusive peace in the Middle East. State University of New York Press. '75.

Lewis, Bernard. The Arabs in history. Harper & Row. '66.

Lucas, Noah. The modern history of Israel. Praeger. '75.

Memmi, Albert. Jews and Arabs. J. P. O'Hara. '75.

Polk, W. R. The United States and the Arab world. Harvard University Press. '75.

* Rikhye, I. J. and Volkmar, John. The Middle East & the new realism. International Peace Academy. 777 United Nations Plaza. New York 10017. '75.

* Vicker, Ray. The kingdom of oil; the Middle East: its people and its power. Scribner. '74.

PERIODICALS

America. 130:433-5. Je. 1, '74. Algeria: third world in microcosm. V. S. Kearney.

Annals of the American Academy of Political and Social Science. 401:64-73. My. '72. American interest in the Palestine question and the establishment of Israel.

Atlantic. 234:6-7+. O. '74. North Africa notebook. Ross Terrill.

Atlantic. 235:6-8+. Ja. '75. Reports & comment: the looming war in the Middle East and how to avoid it. G. W. Ball.

Bulletin of the Atomic Scientists. 31:7-9. Je. '75. What happens when the oil is gone. C. S. Cook.

Business Week. p 78-9+. O. 20, '73. New economics in the Middle East.

Business Week. p 38+. Je. 29, '74. Iran: the superstars of a booming economy.

Business Week. p 104. Jl. 6, '74. More money than Mideast can handle.

Business Week. p 42-3. D. 7, '74. Saudi Arabia: the new breed of empire builders.

* Business Week. p 38-44+. My. 26, '75. Building a new Middle East: special report.

Business Week. p 22-4. Je. 9, '75. Oil producers cool off on nationalization.

Commentary. 57:40-55. F. '74. America, Europe, and the Middle East E. V. Rostow.
   Discussion. Commentary. 18+. Ap; 15-17. My. '74.

Commentary. 58:63-8. D. '74. Conversations in Cairo. Nadav Safran.

Commentary. 59:29-45. Ap. '75. United States & Israel; tilt in the Middle East? Theodore Draper.

Commentary. 59:57-63. My. '75. In search of moderate Egyptians. Joan Peters.

Commonweal. 102:35-6. Ap. 11, '75. Regional arms race.

Commonweal. 102:173-5+. Je. 6, '75. Stand-off in the Middle East; report on a trip to five troubled countries. James O'Gara.

Current History. 68:49-79+. F. '75. Middle East, 1975; symposium.

* Current History. 69:117-20+. O. '75. Soviet policy in the Middle East. O. M. Smolansky.

Department of State Bulletin. 71:295-9. Ag. 19, '74. Middle East: problems and prospects; excerpts from transcript of a University of Chicago roundtable discussion, March 27, 1974. J. J. Sisco.

Forbes. 111:28-30+. F. 15, '73. The nation we'd better get to know [Saudi Arabia].
Editorial comment. Forbes. 111:9. F. 15, '73.

Foreign Affairs. 51:491-504. Ap. '73. Depth of Arab radicalism. Arnold Hottinger.

Foreign Affairs. 53:45-63. O. '74. Engagement in the Middle East. Nadav Safran.

Foreign Affairs. 53:405-31. Ap. '75. New policy for Israel. Stanley Hoffmann.

Foreign Affairs. 53:625-37. Jl. '75. OPEC and the industrial countries: the next ten years. T. O. Enders.

Foreign Affairs. 54:14-35. O. '75. The Persian Gulf: arms race or arms control? E. M. Kennedy.

Foreign Affairs. 54:113-26. O. '75. The psychology of Middle East peace. Nahum Goldmann.

Foreign Affairs. 54:127-33. O. '75. Doomed to peace. Béchir Ben-Yahmed.

Fortune. 90:144-7+. O. '74. Shah drives to build a new Persian empire. Louis Kraar.

Holiday. 50:44-5+. S. '71. Iran: model Middle Eastern state; celebrating its 2,500th anniversary. R. M. Sorge.

Nation. 216:452-3. Ap. 16, '73. Oil for arms.

* Nation. 220:680-4. Je. 7, '75. Egypt rebuilds: boom time along the Suez. Larry Diamond.

National Geographic. 139:834-65. Je. '71. Morocco: land of the farthest west. T. J. Abercrombie.

National Geographic. 147:2-47. Ja. '75. Iran: desert miracle. William Graves.

National Review. 27:211-13+. F. 28, '75. Israel, the Arabs, and oil money. Herbert Cahn.

New Republic. 169:16-21. D. 1, '73. Shah of Iran; interview, ed. by Oriana Fallaci.

New Republic. 171:11-13. Ag. 31, '74. On Israel's east; Arabs of the West Bank. David Pryce-Jones.

New Republic. 172:19-21. F. 22, '75. Interview with King Hussein; ed. by Stanley Karnow.

New Republic. 172:13-16. Mr. 15, '75. At stake for Egypt: food, peace and development. Stanley Karnow.

New Republic. 172:17-19. Ap. 5, '75. Russia's Middle East zigzags. Stanley Karnow.

* New York Post. p 21. F. 7, '76. Lebanon: peace or truce. M. J. Berlin.

New York Times. p 1+. S. 2, '75. Israel and Egypt initial pact on Sinai shifts and use of Suez; a U.S. watch on passes sought. Bernard Gwertzman.

New York Times. p 17. S. 2, '75. Sinai pact separates foes but divides allies. J. M. Markham.

New York Times. p E 4. O. 5, '75. Now Lebanon is taken seriously. Terence Smith.

New York Times. p 19. O. 5, '75. Libya is spending millions of dollars of oil income to promote spread of Islamic faith around the world.

* New York Times. p 3. O. 11, '75. Sinai pact stirs misgivings among Arabs. Henry Tanner.

New York Times. p 1+. O. 26, '75. Crowded and poor, Egypt looking ahead with hope. Henry Tanner.

New York Times. p 3. O. 26, '75. Soviet expands weapons aid to Syria. Drew Middleton.

New York Times. p 3. O. 31, '75. Old order of privilege in Lebanon crumbling in street warfare. J. M. Markham.

* New York Times. p E 2. N. 2, '75. Qaddafi of Libya believes in backing almost any revolution.

New York Times. p 1+. D. 7, '75. Panic grips Beirut amid new killings and kidnappings. J. M. Markham.

New York Times. p E 1. D. 7, '75. Syria plays its Arafat card effectively. J. M. Markham.

New York Times. p E 3. D. 7, '75. How the Palestinians came to be an "issue." Naomi Shepherd.

New York Times. p 1+. Mr. 19, '76. Anarchy in Lebanon; all aspects of society disintegrating as the rival factions battle for power. J. M. Markham.

New York Times Magazine. p 10-11+. F. 6, '72. Colonel Qadhafi, Libya's mystical revolutionary. E. R. F. Sheehan.

New York Times Magazine. p 18-20+. Ap. 23, '72. Algerians intend to go it alone, raise hell, hold out and grow. E. R. F. Sheehan.

New York Times Magazine. p 34-5+. My. 6, '73. Occupation: a sort of social revolution. Amnon Rubinstein.

New York Times Magazine. p 9+. Jl. 15, '73. Sadat is back in his bunker. David Hirst.

New York Times Magazine. p 35+. N. 18, '73. Sadat's war. E. R. F. Sheehan.

Discussion. New York Times Magazine. p 122. D. 9, '73.

New York Times Magazine. p 32-3+. My. 19, '74. Let us begin; dialogue between an Egyptian and an Israeli. Sana Hassan; Amos Elon.

New York Times Magazine. p 9+. My. 26, '74. Shah of shahs, shah of dreams. David Holden.

New York Times Magazine. p 31+. D. 8. '74. Why Sadat and Faisal chose Arafat. E. R. F. Sheehan.

New York Times Magazine. p 20-2+. Ap. 6, '75. Oil or Israel? Louis Harris.

New York Times Magazine. p 13+. My. 18, '75. Wild men become a nation. Ted Morgan.

New York Times Magazine. p 12-13+. Je. 1, '75. Hero of the crossing, they shout, where is our breakfast? David Holden.

New York Times Magazine. p 8-9+. Jl. 6, '75. Family affair: the House of Saud. David Holden.

New York Times Magazine. p 18-19+. S. 14, '75. A sheik who hates to gamble [Yamani]; interview, ed. by Oriana Fallaci.

New York Times Magazine. p 20-2+. N. 9, '75. Cry, Lebanon. J. M. Markham.

New Yorker. 48:78+. F. 10, '73. Letter from Cairo. Joseph Kraft.

New Yorker. 50:92+. Je. 17, '74. Letter from Damascus. Joseph Kraft.

New Yorker. 50:140+. N. 11, '74. Letter from the Middle East. Marilyn Berger.

Newsweek. 81:40-1+. My. 21, '73. Colossus of the oil lanes. Arnaud de Borchgrave.

Newsweek. 82:34-7. S. 10, '73. New politics of Mideast oil.

Newsweek. 85:39-40. Ap. 28, '75. Case of Arab against Arab; fighting between Lebanon's Phalangists and the fedayeen. Raymond Carroll and others.

Newsweek. 86:27-8+. S. 8, '75. The road to peace.

Newsweek. 86:55-6. O. 6, '75. Beirut: patriotic gore. N. C. Proffitt.

Newsweek. 86:42-3. O. 20, '75. On the brink of civil war. Kim Willenson and others.

* Newsweek. 86:55-6+. D. 15, '75. The PLO: coming on strong. M. R. Benjamin and others.

Reader's Digest. 103:193-7. N. '73. Qaddafi of Libya; the big question mark in oil. David Reed.

Reader's Digest. 106:72-6. F. '75. It's our move in the Middle East. W. E. Griffith.

Saturday Evening Post. 243:46-7. Fall '71. Iran: ancient and ageless. R. M. Sorge.

Saturday Evening Post. 247:18+. Ap. '75. King Hussein: monarch in the middle. C. M. Stegmuller.

Saturday Evening Post. 247:38-9+. O. '75. Seven steps to peace in the Middle East. F. R. Barnett.

Time. 98:26-8. Jl. 26, '71. Morocco: the cracked facade.

Time. 99:23-4. Je. 19, '72. Colonizers: Israeli settlements on occupied territory.

Time. 101:23-6+. Ap. 2,' 73. Arab world; oil, power, violence.

* Time. 104:28-33+. N. 4, '74. Oil, grandeur and a challenge to the West.

Time. 105:24-8+. Ja. 6, '75. Desert king faces the modern world.

Time. 105:26+. F. 10, '75. View from two generations [interviews with Feisal and Boumedienne].

Time. 105:32+. My. 19, '75. End to isolation.

Travel. 144:38-43+. Ag. '75. Lebanon: land of milk & honey. Linda Blackwood.

U.S. News & World Report. 72:67-8. Ja. 3, '72. Arab friend of the U.S. fights to stay in power.

U.S. News & World Report. 74:40-3. My. 28, '73. Oil: real stake for U.S. in Mideast? [Arabs' views vs. Israelis' views] J. Law; J. Fromm.

U.S. News & World Report. 75:28-9. Ag. 6, '73. As Libya flexes muscles in the Arab world . . .

U.S. News & World Report. 75:65-6. Ag. 6, '73. Arab oil money piles up; a burden or a blessing?

U.S. News & World Report. 76:60-2. Ja. 14, '74. Arabs and their money; a lot of ways to spend it.

U.S. News & World Report. 78:47-8. Ja. 20, '75. When the Suez Canal reopens—bonanza for Egypt, others too.

U.S. News & World Report. 78:49-50+. Mr. 10, '75. Persian Gulf: where big powers are playing a risky game.

U.S. News & World Report. 78:31-2. Mr. 24, '75. Behind the Mideast talks, U.S.-Soviet struggle goes on.

U.S. News & World Report. 79:53-5. Ag. 25, '75. Iraq turns sour on Russia, and it's the U.S. that gains. Dennis Mullin.

U.S. News & World Report. 79:19-21. S. 1, '75. High cost to the U.S. of an agreement in the Mideast.

U.S. News & World Report. 79:14-15. S. 8, '75. Breakthrough in Mideast—U.S. takes on controversial role.

UNESCO Courier. 23:34-41. D. '70. Tunis: a jewel of Islam. Georges Fradier.

Vital Speeches of the Day. 41:331-5. Mr. 15, '75. Energy and the Middle East; address, February 13, 1975. J. W. Fulbright.

* Vital Speeches of the Day. 41:647-50. Ag. 15, '75. New dimensions in the Middle East; address, June 16, 1975. L. D. Brown.

* Wall Street Journal. p 1+. N. 24, '75. Arab oil money backs Sudan's development as prime food source. Ray Vicker.

Shelter State